Improving Your
Emotional Intelligence
Workbook

A Competency-Based Approach to Understanding, Applying, and
Recognizing the Benefits of EI in the Workplace

First Edition 2022

ISBN: 9798412181400

Centrestar Learning
State College, Pennsylvania, USA
www.centrestar.com

Endorsements for Improving Your Emotional Intelligence

"This common-sense guidebook helps you identify your EI competencies, build them into strengths, and helps you in your pursuit of your life's goals and objectives. The workbook contains assessments to help you focus on your strengths —at the end of each section are simple and practical action items that allow you to start making progress immediately —then, at the end of the workbook is a checklist of 30 actions and strategies that you can pursue to apply what you learn. These actions and strategies will help you to dramatically improve your self-awareness and empathy. The mastery of EI competencies is so greatly needed in our ever-changing, faced paced work and life environment. If you want to be a better person, supervisor, or leader you need to read this book."

— Dr. Patricia Macko,
Senior OD, Learning and Development Specialist, Geisinger Health System, Danville, PA

"So often, our emotions can derail otherwise successful workplace experiences. Improving Your Emotional Intelligence succinctly explains how to develop a plan for managing emotions by applying what you learn throughout the concepts presented in this practical competency-based workbook. The "hands-on" approach includes assessments to focus your learning and activities leading to the development of your action plan. This is a great book for young professionals new in their careers or seasoned veterans hoping to maximize the positive benefits of EI in any work environment."

— Dr. Michele Newhard,
Talent Development Specialist, Colorado State University; Principal, Polaris Pathways, Ltd.
Gallup Certified Strengths Coach; Certified Life & Mentor Coach, Fort Collins, CO

"Emotional Intelligence (EQ) has become an important issue as work shifts from residential environments to all online or hybrid environments. Supervisors, managers, and executives must learn how to interact effectively with people, and the new work environments now make EQ a topic of special importance. This book helps readers identify their EQ and, when used in an organization, raise the general level of EQ. That is all the more important as so many workers complain of feelings of isolations and suicide rates skyrocket in the U.S. and globally."

— Dr. William J. Rothwell,
Distinguished Professor, Department of Learning & Performance Systems,
Penn State University, University Park, PA

"Emotional Intelligence (EI) continues to be one of the most important elements of a successful business and its people. The current global pandemic has proven the continued desire from the workforce to put the people-side of the business at its core. The reality is that organizations must embrace and celebrate an EI mindset to attract, engage and retain top talent. Improving Your Emotional Intelligence is a must-have practical workbook that provides tools, exercises, and assessments that help build a powerful set of emotional intelligence competencies."

— Dr. Leila Farzam,
Subject Matter Expert, REI Systems, Inc., Washington DC

Improving Your
Emotional Intelligence
Workbook

A Competency-Based Approach to Understanding, Applying, and Recognizing the Benefits of EI in the Workplace

*"CEOs are hired for their intellect and business expertise –
and fired for a lack of emotional intelligence."*
— *Daniel Goleman*

Preface

I'm sure you know people who, despite being knowledgeable and technically proficient, can't seem to work well with others. They may be insensitive, excessively argumentative, dismissive of people with opinions contrary to theirs, easily angered. Or, they may become "unhinged" when dealing with a challenging or stressful situation. As bosses, their behavior contributes to high stress, low-satisfaction work environments, where employees feel undervalued and, most likely, under-developed. While such people may have high IQ's, they are low in emotional intelligence.

Emotional Intelligence is a different way of being smart. It includes a few competencies that help us with self-management and interacting effectively with others. It is a strong factor in determining success as a leader and in other life roles. Emotional intelligence is more than keeping one's emotions under control: it includes knowing how emotion, cognition, and behavior— feeling, thinking and acting—influence each other. Research into how the brain responds when we have an emotionally arousing event is giving us a better understanding of what is a complex process, involving several physical areas of the brain, and triggering a number of feelings, thoughts and actions.

As well as increasing your awareness of your own emotional intelligence, this workbook will give you a good, general understanding of the characteristics common to emotionally intelligent people. The concept reviews and application activities provide insight into what we, as human beings, think and do in emotionally charged situations and how our emotions can be managed to better advantage. Even so, the focus is clearly on self-understanding: how well you know yourself, emotionally; how well you use your emotions to positive ends; what you need to understand and manage better; and, how you can develop your emotional competencies.

As you complete the readings and activities, you will put together an emotional intelligence development plan to guide your continued learning. This is an especially important tool for improving emotional intelligence. As adults, we are experienced in developing our knowledge and learning new skills: it's part of everyday life. It is important, however, to note that developing emotional intelligence can present some challenges not associated with other types of learning. It requires, first, a recognition of the benefits of such development, then a willingness to surface and question the feeling-thinking-behaving routines that we developed over time. That is, we may have to "unlearn" patterned behaviors that we believe have served us well, and replace them with more positive, adaptive choices. Your development plan will guide you through these critical steps.

Drs. Wesley E. Donahue
and Katheryn K. Woodley
2022

Acknowledgments

We did not create this workbook alone, and I want to acknowledge the people who contributed significantly to the work: Drs. Lisa Donahue and Rebecca Sarnaski for their invaluable research efforts in tracking down articles, books, and other sources needed for content development and identifying examples; Lisa Donahue and Billie Tomlinson for their editing and attention to detail; Valentine Platon for adding graphics that help bring the text to life; Alex Donahue and Zizi Iryaspraha Subiyarta for thoughtful design suggestions; Amit Dey for text formatting; and former instructors and professional associates at Penn State Management who shared their business and industry wisdom and years of teaching experience; the individuals who took the time to review the manuscript; and the many thousands of people who participated in surveys, focus groups, and interviews, without whom this workbook would lack the richness of real-world detail. To all these people I offer a sincere and heartfelt Thank you!

"Emotional Intelligence grows through perception. Look around at your present situation and observe it through the level of feeling."

— Deepak Chopra

Structured Learning Design

All our workbooks align with our research-based **Competency Model.** The model, which is rooted in work by the U.S. Department of Labor and others, gives you a framework for structured learning by helping you identify and develop specific competencies.

If you ask people to define competency, you may be amazed at the variety of responses you receive. We define a *competency* as a set of skills, knowledge, attitudes, and behaviors that are observable and measurable. *The emphasis here is on observable and measurable.* It is not enough that you *think* you are competent in an area. You must be able to *behave* in ways that demonstrate your competence to others.

Our framework has **35 competency dimensions** associated with successful performance in leadership and professional roles.

Centrestar Competency Model

Based on thousands of business participant responses from many industries, we clustered these 35 competencies into five competency domains, which we named and coded as follows:

    A. Resource Management
    B. Professional Competence
    C. Supervisory/Management
    D. Organizational Leadership
    E. Technical Acumen

Competencies and clusters may overlap, but for each workbook we identify the three competencies with which the content is most closely associated. Our **Improving Your Emotional Intelligence** workbook focuses on the competency areas of **Self-Responsibility and Management, Interpersonal Skills**, and **Interpersonal Relationship Building**. The content is most associated with the **Professional Competence** competency cluster, as shown below.

A. RESOURCE MANAGEMENT
_____ 1. Computer and Literacy Skills
_____ 2. Technical Competence
_____ 3. Resource Usage
_____ 4. Resource Management
_____ 5. Understands Systems

B. PROFESSIONAL COMPETENCE
_____ 6. Conceptual Thinking
_____ 7. Learning and Information Skills
__X__ 8. Self-Responsibility and Management
__X__ 9. Interpersonal Skills
_____ 10. Oral Communication
_____ 11. Written Communication

D. ORGANIZATIONAL LEADERSHIP
_____ 22. Human Performance Management
_____ 23. Planning and Evaluation
_____ 24. Financial Management and Budgeting
_____ 25. Technology Management
_____ 26. Creative Thinking
_____ 27. Vision
_____ 28. External Awareness
_____ 29. Strategic Thinking and Planning
_____ 30. Management Controls
_____ 31. Diverse Workforce
_____ 32. Leading Change

Centrestar Competency Model

C. SUPERVISORY MANAGEMENT
_____ 12. Leadership and Coaching
_____ 13. Flexibility and Resilience
_____ 14. Problem Solving
_____ 15. Decisiveness
_____ 16. Self-Direction
_____ 17. Conflict Management
_____ 18. Teamwork and Cooperation
_____ 19. Influencing and Negotiating
_____ 20. Customer Focus
__X__ 21. Interpersonal Relationship Building

E. TECHNICAL ACUMEN
_____ 33. Job-Specific Competencies
_____ 34. Occupational Competencies
_____ 35. Industry-Wide Competencies

How to Use this Workbook

This workbook is structured to be a hands-on guide with options for how you can use the material.

One way to use the workbook is to read it straight through. Or you can jump to specific sections depending on your interests and goals. We recommend you start by reviewing the table of contents, so you understand the workbook's organization. Read the overview, and then take the introductory assessment by rating your level of agreement with the ten statements. This will help you clarify your current thinking. After that, scan the workbook. Scanning will help you pinpoint areas where you may have an information gap and areas where feel confident. From there, you can set your learning goals and dive deeper into the material.

The workbook will help you develop your competence by addressing the ten most vital concepts associated with a topical area. The content for the ten concepts is structured in a consistent learning format.

Each concept starts with several paragraphs of relevant content and ends with three **What to Do** action suggestions, followed by a **Remember** section which lists important learning points. To **Enhance Your Learning**, we offer links to additional resources. Each concept area concludes with a **Reinforce Your Learning** application activity.

At the end of workbook is a **Summary** and a **Recap Checklist**. The recap lists all the 30 **What to Do** actions from each concept in the workbook.

A 20-question **Knowledge Review Test** is also available with answers. You can use it to test your knowledge, or it is an optional feature for those who seek to earn development hours (4 hrs.) to maintain their professional credentials. For more information about professional development hours, visit our website at www.centrestar.com.

As with most things in life, **you will get out of this workbook only what you put into it.** To learn and grow you must engage fully with the material presented. Ask yourself questions as you read the material in the workbook. Do the activities and answer the questions in each concept? Make notes. Look for ideas new to you and consider how they fit with your current knowledge. Recognize what you already know and can build on, and what might be a new way of looking at something.

This workbook aims to ensure that your skills are at the highest level they can be. Engaging with the concepts and materials will help you become a more rounded professional who experiences success in your chosen career.

"The strength of character and emotional intelligence to face your failures and learn from them are at the core of success."

— - Robert Kiyosaki

Contents

"You can conquer almost any fear if you will only make up your mind to do so. For remember, fear doesn't exist anywhere except in the mind."

— Dale Carnegie

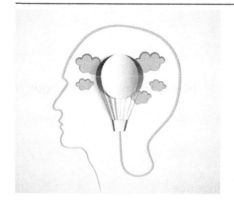

Overview

"Our feelings are not there to be cast out or conquered. They're there to be engaged and expressed with imagination and intelligence."

- T.K. Coleman, author

People are intelligent in many different ways, and in today's highly interactive, team-based workplaces, being emotionally intelligent is regarded as an increasingly significant competence and has definite advantages. It is critical to building and maintaining healthy workplace relationships with others, and for thriving in high pressure or high change situations.

Some research findings indicate that emotional intelligence, abbreviated as **EI** or **EQ**, may account for **58% of your success in life**, professional and private. In spite of how important it is, one study found that only **36% of people** studied were emotionally intelligent enough to recognize their emotional state (Van Camp, 2015). And, in another study examining how emotional intelligence and IQ affect performance, the **lower IQ** person **outperformed** the higher IQ person **seven out of ten times** if the person with the lower IQ had **higher emotional intelligence** (Bradberry, 2014).

Success in life

only 36% of people studied were emotionally intelligent enough to recognize their emotional state

This workbook focuses on increasing your understanding of what emotional intelligence is, how it affects workplace behavior, and how it contributes to one's success and contentment. As you work through the concepts, you will be examining different aspects of emotional intelligence and putting together a plan to continue developing your EI awareness and skills.

After completing this workbook, you should be able to:

- Recognize the benefits of EI in the workplace

- Increase your emotional self-awareness, emotional regulation, social awareness, and ability to navigate relationships

- Realize how negative and positive emotions drive workplace behavior and the overall climate

- Identify your EI strengths and areas for development

- Build an action plan to strengthens your EI competencies

The competencies associated with this workbook include:

| Self-Responsibility and Management | Interpersonal Skills | Interpersonal Relationship Building |

Take Your Temperature for Improving Your Emotional Intelligence

With yourself and your organization in mind, read each statement carefully. Next to each statement, write the number (from 1 to 10) that indicates your level of agreement with the statement.

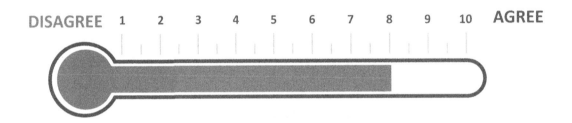

DISAGREE 1   2   3   4   5   6   7   8   9   10   AGREE

_____ 1.   I understand the concept of Emotional Intelligence and its benefits.

_____ 2.   I understand how the brain processes emotions.

_____ 3.   I understand how positive and negative emotions affect behavior.

_____ 4.   I have a good understanding of my Emotional Intelligence competencies.

_____ 5.   I describe myself as highly emotionally self-aware.

_____ 6.   I have excellent skills in regulating my emotions.

_____ 7.   I am good at reading the emotions of other people.

_____ 8.   I can help and support others in managing their emotions.

_____ 9.   I know what the key social intelligence skills are, and their importance.

_____ 10. I know how to support an emotionally positive work climate.

_____ **Total**

What challenges have you or your organization experienced related to the emotions of people in the workplace?

_____

_____

_____

_____

_____

_____

_____

_____

Take a few minutes to reflect on the "temperature" of your Emotional Intelligence self-assessment and consider 2 or 3 areas that you would like to develop or improve upon:

_____

_____

_____

_____

_____

_____

_____

_____

_____

_____

_____

_____

As you progress through this workbook consider what actions you can take to demonstrate competence in the following three competency areas:

1. **Self-Responsibility and Management** – displays responsibility, self-confidence, emotional self-control, integrity, and honesty

2. **Interpersonal Skills –** appropriately sociable; interacts effectively with others

3. **Interpersonal Relationship Building** – considers and responds appropriately to the needs, feelings, and capabilities of others; seeks feedback and accurately assesses impact on others; provides helpful feedback; builds trust with others

Define Emotional Intelligence and Understand Its Benefits

Most of us have known people, through our work or personal associations, who appear very bright and knowledgeable in a technical or fact-based sense, but who are challenged when it comes to handling difficult situations or relating to others. They may behave in ways that seem inconsiderate, uncaring, or rude. Or, they may be quick to anger or easily upset over situations that others can handle with ease. While they may have high **IQ's** –the traditional measure of human intelligence – they may be falling short in **EI –emotional intelligence**.

Emotional intelligence has been widely researched since the early 1990's and has been shown to be critical to success in work and life in general. The term itself implies both feeling and thought, with a focus on the importance of emotions as the first screen for all information received. Research has found it to be a better predictor of success than relevant work experience and IQ which, in some studies, accounted for only 4 to 25% of the variance (Cherniss, 2000). When the careers of bright, well-educated and experienced leaders derail, it is largely because of difficulty in adapting to change and the inability to work well with others (Cherniss, 1999; Cherniss, 2000 Goleman, 1998; Stein & others, 2009).

Daniel Goleman, whose research and publications on EI have contributed significantly to our understanding of the concepts, **defines EI as "the capacity for recognizing our own feelings and those of others, for motivating ourselves, and for managing emotions well in ourselves and in our relationships."** (Goleman, 1998). Just as IQ is a capacity that allows us to develop various intellectual skills and competencies, EQ is the foundation for developing emotional competence: the skills of self-awareness, emotional regulation and understanding and connecting with others. These are the personal and social skills that lead to superior performance in the world of work.

Goleman's model consists of four dimensions of EI, as shown below. The competencies associated with each dimension are discussed in later sections of the workbook.

	PERSONAL	SOCIAL
Awareness	Self-Awareness	Social Awareness
Actions	Self-Management	Relationship Management

Because of the specific competencies Goleman has identified, his model fits very well when considering how emotional intelligence affects the quality of relationships and performance at work. Other models have similar dimensions but somewhat different competencies. Salovey and Mayer, who coined the term "emotional intelligence," defined it as "a form of social intelligence that involves the ability to monitor one's own and others' feelings and emotions, to discriminate among them, and to use this information to guide one's thinking and action" (Cherniss, 2000).

Following are some important things to keep in mind about the nature and importance of emotional intelligence:

Emotional Intelligence is not about: being "nice" all the time or openly sharing all your feelings with everyone. It is not a "once in a while" type of thing or, a fixed, static capacity. It is also not about denying or suppressing your emotions so that they don't affect your behavior.

Emotional Intelligence: is a different way of being smart; a strong factor in determining success as a leader and in other life roles; the capacity for developing a number of important personal and interpersonal competencies. "Emotional intelligence is an assortment of mental abilities and skills that can help you to successfully manage both yourself and the demands of working with others" (Walton, 2012).

Emotional intelligence is more than keeping one's emotions under control: it includes knowing when and how to express emotion, including the ability to handle stress.

Although there are different theories about the components of emotional intelligence, there is general agreement that the EI competencies are **largely learned and continue to develop as we go through life.**

People with high levels of emotional self-awareness and self-management are able to identify specific emotions—such as anger, fear, joy or sadness – as they are being felt. They are aware of their emotional triggers and understand how their emotions affect their behavior. Rather than being "out of control" when experiencing a negative emotion, such as anger, or suppressing it, they are able to find appropriate ways to express it. Either extreme—losing control or suppressing a legitimate emotion—can negatively affect both relationships and one's physical and mental health.

The social aspects of emotional intelligence are also important: the ability to understand how others are feeling –in the moment—improves our ability to communicate with them and gives us clues about how we can provide them comfort or support and work more effectively with them.

Compared with people low in emotional intelligence, emotionally intelligent people:

- Are better able to handle difficult, demanding situations,

- Have better quality work relationships,

- Express their ideas and preferences better, and have greater influence

- Are more admired and respected by others

- Are more likely to move into positions of leadership,

- Are more productive, and,

- Are generally more satisfied and happier with their lives.

What to do:	Other actions:
☐ Pay attention to how you respond to difficult or challenging interactions or work situations.	☐ _____ ☐ _____
☐ Pay attention to how your co-workers respond when things are not going well.	☐ _____ ☐ _____
☐ Consider how important emotional intelligence is in your workplace, and whether or not it is evident in workplace interactions.	☐ _____ ☐ _____

Remember

✓ Emotional intelligence involves the personal competencies of recognizing and managing our emotions, and the social competencies of recognizing others' emotions and managing our relationships.

✓ Emotional self-awareness means you can identify an emotion at the time it is experienced and understand how the emotion affects your behavior.

✓ Emotions are the natural, normal responses to events and greatly influence our thinking and behavior.

Enhance Your Learning

Watch the following 5-minute video by Daniel Goleman to learn more about what emotional intelligence is, and consider how you can apply this information in your work:

Big Think. (2012). *Daniel Goleman Introduces Emotion Intelligence.*		Available at: https://www.youtube.com/watch?v=Y7m9eNoB3NU

Reinforce Your Learning

Understanding EI.

1. Take a moment to write your own definition of emotional intelligence.
   Emotional intelligence is:

_____

_____

_____

_____

_____

_____

_____

_____

_____

_____

_____

_____

_____

_____

_____

_____

2. Do a web search and read two or three other definitions. Compare these with the definitions given in this course, and your own definition. Make any changes in your original definition, so that you are comfortable answering the question, "what is emotional intelligence?"

3. What do you most want to better understand about emotional intelligence and how it relates to success and contentment? Consider this the first step in your EI Awareness and Development Plan.

"When dealing with people, remember you are not dealing with creatures of logic, but with creatures of emotion."

- Dale Carnegie

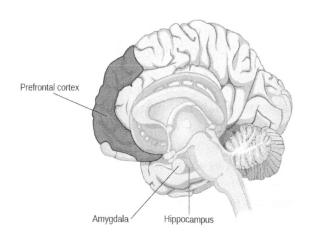

Prefrontal cortex

Amygdala   Hippocampus

Understand How the Brain Processes Emotions

Emotions typically arise in response to a specific event, either internal or external, that has meaning for the individual. The meaning can be positive or negative and is highly individual as it is linked to one's earlier life experiences.

An emotion is more than just a feeling. Daniel Goleman has defined emotion as follows:

"I take emotion to refer to a feeling and its distinctive thoughts, psychological and biological states, and range of propensities to act" **(Goleman, 1995 p 189).** Emotion, cognition and behavior— feeling, thinking and acting—influence each other. Each emotion can affect, among other things, our level of physiological arousal, our motor responses, and how we interact with others. For example, common responses to sadness include crying and withdrawal from others, and responses to anger include reddening of the face and verbally or physically aggressive behavior.

Research into how the brain responds when we have an emotionally arousing event is giving us a better understanding of what is a complex process, involving several physical areas of the brain, and triggering a number of feelings, thoughts and actions. For example, when you are walking through a dark parking lot and suddenly hear footsteps rapidly approaching from behind, your emotional response is likely to be fear. You will also respond with thoughts – "should I look back?" – "can I get to my car in time?" – or "I need to defend myself." Your heart rate will increase, and a number of other physiological changes will be triggered, preparing you to take action. And all this happens very quickly.

Following are some important things to keep in mind about how the brain processes emotions:

Recent research has included mapping the physical locations of various brain functions. We now understand that the different parts of our brain have different characteristics, and even though they influence each other, they can also operate independently. Translated, when we experience anger, we can react impulsively and defensively with verbal abusiveness even though our "brain" knows that there are more appropriate language choices.

The two main brain systems of interest in emotional intelligence are the limbic system and the cerebral cortex. The limbic system, which includes the **amygdala**, is deeper within the temporal lobes of the brain and develops before the higher-level cerebral system, the **prefrontal cortex**.

When an emotionally significant event occurs, information is carried from the sense organs to the thalamus, which registers what we have seen, heard, tasted or touched. (The sense of smell can also arouse emotions but affects a different part of the brain.) The thalamus sends nerve impulses in two directions: to the amygdala, in the limbic system, and through the **hippocampus** to the prefrontal cortex. The path to the amygdala is shorter and more direct than the path to the cortex, so the amygdala receives the message first. As the storehouse of memories of emotional reactions, it takes a snapshot of the incoming message and compares it with stored earlier scenes. If it finds a match between the incoming message and a fearful or hurtful stored memory, it then triggers the hypothalamus to initiate the physical changes that accompany emotions and stimulate motor areas of the brain.

Meanwhile the message travels through the hippocampus, part of the limbic system that plays an important role in consolidating information for long term memory, to the prefrontal cortex. The pre-frontal cortex, which stores long-term memory, processes the incoming message in a relatively slow, careful, analytical manner. It then sends its interpretation of the event back to the amygdala which influences how we respond emotionally and behaviorally.

Because the limbic system responds more quickly –and impulsively—than the cortex, an event can elicit an emotional reaction and a motor response before the person has even begun to think about what the event means. Although the reaction time difference may be just a fraction of a second, the quicker response of the limbic system can cause someone to behave impulsively even when he or she has the cognitive ability to choose a more adaptive response.

The amygdala triggers quick, crude emotional reactions. Its firing excites us and pushes us to take action. Applying a basic emotional intelligence tool, naming your feelings as they are experienced, reduces the rate of amygdala firing and produces a calming effect. It gives you more time to consciously choose your response.

Automatic Responses. As we experience different emotionally arousing situations, we respond by thinking, feeling and acting. Over time, we lay down neural tracks that quickly connect the events to the responses. The neural connections that support these are strengthened, becoming dominant pathways for nerve impulses. Connections that are unused become weakened, while those that people use over and over grow increasingly strong, creating a habitual pattern. With sufficient repetition, the neural circuitry becomes almost "hard wired:" the brain knows what to do and takes us through the habitual response without being told. The thoughts, feelings and actions happen automatically and quickly, often with the person having little awareness of making choices. The automatic response, a habitual repertoire of thought, feeling and action, is learned. Fortunately, **new neural tracks can be created and doing so is a significant part of developing emotional intelligence.**

"Emotional competencies combine thought and feeling. … The tight orchestration of thought and feeling is made possible by what amounts to a superhighway in the brain—a bundle of neurons connecting the prefrontal lobes, behind the forehead—the brain's executive decision-making center—with an area deep in the brain that harbors our emotions" (Goleman, 1998 pp 23-24).

What to do:	Other actions:
☐ Choose one emotion, such as anger or joy, and think about your behavior when feeling that emotion.	☐ _____ ☐ _____
☐ Identify a situation in which you responded automatically and a situation in which you consciously chose your response. How were the results different?	☐ _____ ☐ _____ ☐ _____
☐ Identify one or mechanisms you use for calming down when emotions are getting out of control.	☐ _____ ☐ _____

Remember

✓ Emotions typically arise in response to a specific event, either internal or external, that has meaning for the individual.

✓ An emotion includes feelings, thoughts, psychological and biological states and action tendencies.

✓ The quicker response of the limbic system can cause someone to behave impulsively even when he or she has the cognitive ability to choose a more adaptive response.

✓ You can learn to apply an emotional intelligence tool and more consciously choose your response.

Enhance Your Learning

Watch the 7-minute video by Small Business Answers, "Amygdala Hijacking – Don't Let it Happen to You," and consider how you can apply the concepts to enhance your emotional intelligence.

Small Business Answers. (2009). *Amygdala Hijacking – Don't Let it Happen to You.*		Available at: https://www.youtube.com/watch?v=YM3cXZ7CFls

Reinforce your learning

Increase awareness of "automatic" routines.

1. To the extent that you can, describe your "typical" thought, feeling, and action responses to situations that elicit the following emotions:

Anger:

Joy:

Sadness:

Fear:

2. If you can, describe your earliest memory of that emotion.

Describe How Positive and Negative Emotions Affect Behavior

It is not when things are going well that defines the power of emotional intelligence; it's when things aren't going well.

In his first book about emotional intelligence, Goleman described EI as a master aptitude:

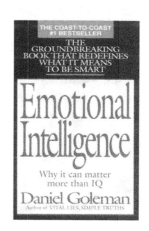

"To the degree that our emotions get in the way of or enhance our ability to think and plan, to pursue training for a distant goal, to solve problems and the like, they define the limits of our capacity to use our innate mental abilities, and so determine how we do in life. And to the degree to which we are motivated by feelings of enthusiasm and pleasure in what we do—or even by an optimal degree of anxiety— they propel us to accomplishment. It is in this sense that emotional intelligence is a master aptitude, a capacity that profoundly affects all other abilities, either facilitating or interfering with them" (Goleman, 1995).

There are several different lists of emotions, but there is general agreement that there are a few basic ones that can be combined and configured in different magnitudes to produce additional emotions or mood states. Paul Ekman, psychologist and leading researcher on emotions and facial expression, identified six basic emotions that he found to be similarly expressed in different cultures: fear, sadness, anger, happiness (or joy), surprise, and disgust. Extending beyond the basic six, the following is a typical, but not exhaustive, list of common human emotions (About Human Emotions, 2016):

Acceptance	Contempt	Frustration	Hunger	Rage
Affection	Depression	Gratitude	Hysteria	Regret
Aggression	Doubt	Grief	Interest	Remorse
Ambivalence	Ecstasy	Guilt	Loneliness	Shame
Apathy	Empathy	Hatred	Love	Suffering
Anxiety	Envy	Hope	Paranoia	Sympathy
Boredom	Embarrassment	Horror	Pity	
Compassion	Euphoria	Hostility	Pleasure	
Confusion	Forgiveness	Homesickness	Pride	

Some lists include jealousy and resentment along with its listed relief, satisfaction, helplessness, excitement and disappointment as emotion-related or ambiguous mood states.

Following are some important things to keep in mind about how positive and negative emotions affect behavior:

Some emotions or mood states contribute positively to our ability to work effectively with others. These positive emotions or **higher mood states i**nclude, for example: kindness, appreciation, compassion, patience, gratitude and enjoyment. Negative emotions, the **lower mood states**, can compromise our ability to interact authentically and respectfully with others. These include frustration, boredom, anxiety, anger, and hostility. If frequent, these lower mood states or emotions can jeopardize the quality of a work relationship and lead to a breakdown of trust and caring.

When we are in the higher mood states, we tend to be more open to and accepting of others—even when their behavior is challenging. It is easier to be a good coach or team player, and we are more open and accepting of change. In the lower mood states, we are not as effective at such things as coaching, collaborating with others, solving problems, resolving conflicts, or showing consideration to others. Our thoughts are unreliable. We tend to misinterpret events and see others in a negative light. It is easier to believe that someone else's actions were intentionally made to hurt or irritate us, thus easier to become upset with that person.

The negative emotions or mood states are elicited when our sense receptors perceive that we are at risk or in danger. The danger can be external, such as coming across a large bear as you walk through the woods, or internal, such as a sudden worry that a relationship is falling apart. The amygdala's message to the hypothalamus in both events is "prepare this person to survive." This sets in motion the stress response, also known as the **fight, flight or freeze response.**

The stress response is actually a complex set of responses, involving high levels of physiological arousal designed to prepare the body for physical endurance and survival. This level of arousal also disrupts our ability to engage in complex thinking. The hormones triggered as part of the stress response, adrenaline, noradrenaline and cortisol, do an excellent job of preparing us to meet a physical challenge. They increase our heart rate, sharpen our senses, quicken our reaction times and lower our sensitivity to pain. Unfortunately, they are counterproductive if what we're dealing with is a threat to our status at work or a troubled relationship. In essence, they disrupt our emotional self-regulation, planning and reasoning. When we're angry, anxious or afraid, we, literally, neurologically, can't think straight. Our deeply imprinted emotional memories lead us to respond habitually, as we learned long ago, without thinking.

Fight, flight or freeze obliterates emotional intelligence.

The prefrontal lobes of the brain exert some control over the surges of the amygdala. As the analytical, thinking part of the brain, it sorts out the details of the situation and, if we are not really at risk, sends that message back to the amygdala. As we reviewed in concept 2, the problem with negative emotions is that by the time the prefrontal lobes become active, the alarm signal has been sent out. Even though the processing done in the prefrontal lobes is more complete and more realistic, if the alarm signal has been sent, our emotions—even irrational ones—tend to take charge, overpowering the ability of the prefrontal lobes to come up with more rational responses. The mind and body tend to become locked into a recurring pattern, where the emotional arousal can flood us with stress hormones and irrational fear, anxiety or anger. The internal reactions often result in repeating old unhealthy and ineffective patterns of speech and action. The impact on our relationships can be harmful and even disastrous.

To manage our responses to our deeply imprinted emotional memories we need to be aware of our strong emotions **as they are rising and before acting or speaking.** Taking a step back and calming ourselves will give our prefrontal lobes a chance to catch up with the alarm signals being sent by the amygdala, so that we can do a better job of analyzing the situation before responding. But we have to recognize the benefits of doing so, and that is not always the case. This is not a new concept. Consider, for example, the words of a mid-20th century philosopher:

> "In reality we have much more power over negative emotions than we think, particularly when we already know how dangerous they are and how urgent is the struggle with them. But we find too many excuses for them, and swim in the seas of self-pity and selfishness, as the case may be, finding fault in everything except ourselves. (Ouspensky, 1954)

According to leading researcher Barbara Fredrickson, negative emotions are behaviorally predictive (Fredrickson, 2000, 2013):

- **Anger**: fight, hurt, defeat, kill.
- **Fear**: run, avoid, prevent harm.
- **Despair**: freeze, play dead, survive by passivity.

Positive emotions function differently from negative emotions, signaling "safety" rather than "danger." By doing so, according to Fredrickson's **broaden and build theory** they expand the number of choices we have for thinking and behaving and allow us to develop resources we can draw upon in the future. By broadening our momentary thought-action repertoires, we can become healthier: more knowledgeable, creative, resilient, and socially integrated. Her top ten positive emotions are: joy, pride, amusement, serenity, gratitude, hope, interest, awe, inspiration and love (Fredrickson, 2013). Positive emotions are associated with greater attention span and working memory, enhanced verbal fluency, greater openness to information and reduced anxiety.

The brain's response to positive emotions has not been studied as much as the negative emotions, so we are not sure of the exact mechanisms and what the effects are on our thinking and acting. However, it is clear that hormone secretions of endorphins, dopamine and serotonin affect our experience of pleasure as well as our learning and memory.

In mental life, thinking and feeling –cognition and emotions– are interwoven. This is especially true when we are involved in complex decision-making and interacting with other people. What we say to ourselves, consciously or otherwise, affects how we feel. If you think, for example, that you will not be able to handle an assignment, this is an internal event likely to trigger a negative emotional response: fear, shame or helplessness. If you think of the assignment as a challenging learning opportunity, the emotional responses triggered may be inspiration or interest. These lead to different behaviors. If your first thought is, "I cannot possibly do this," and you pull back, think about what you have accomplished before, and change your thoughts to "this will be interesting," you are using emotional intelligence to move from a negative to a positive emotional state.

Our thoughts strongly affect how happy, hopeful and contented we are on a day-to-day basis. There is also evidence from longitudinal research, where people are tracked across decades, that positive thoughts affect our health. (Peterson & others, 1988).

Positive psychology is a field of inquiry that focuses on what is good, pleasurable and right in the human experience, psychologically speaking. It promotes positive emotions and supports emotional regulation. One key characteristics of a positive psychological orientation is an optimistic thinking pattern. People with an optimistic thinking pattern look at the upside of things and this prompts more positive emotions. Those with a pessimistic pattern look at the downside, provoking more negative emotions. Optimism is also a base requirement for resilience, the ability to absorb high levels of disruptive change and continue to function effectively: meet responsibilities, make difficult decisions, and interact with others in respectful ways.

What to do:	**Other actions:**
☐ Whenever you are in a non-physically threatening situation and sense a negative emotion, pull back and give yourself time to think of explanations that lead to more positive emotional responses.	☐ _____ ☐ _____ ☐ _____ ☐ _____
☐ Work with another person to positively resolve a conflict, provide feedback, or solve a problem.	☐ _____ ☐ _____
☐ Know whether you're in response to a challenge tends to be more optimistic or pessimistic.	☐ _____ ☐ _____

Remember

✓ Positive emotions function differently from negative emotions, signaling "safety" rather than "danger."

✓ To move from pessimism to optimism, negative to positive emotions, identify your pessimistic thoughts (e.g., this is impossible) and replace with more optimistic views (e.g., I can learn from this).

✓ Fredrickson's Principle: Negative emotions (fear, anger, despair) help up survive; Positive emotions (curiosity, delight, interest, joy etc.) let us thrive. (Fredrickson, 2013)

Enhance Your Learning

Watch the following 3-minute video to learn more about how emotions affect behavior and consider how you can apply this information to enhance your emotional intelligence.

Gouvenia, B. (2013). *Emotional Intelligence.*		Available at: https://www.youtube.com/watch?v=weuLejJdUu0

Reinforce Your Learning

A. "Losing it – emotionally." Think about a recent interpersonal situation where your emotions interfered with attaining a result or outcome you wanted. Choose a situation that involves you and one other person.

1. Who else was involved and what is his or her relationship to you? (co-worker, manager, friend, family member, neighbor, etc.)

2. Briefly describe what transpired: How did the event start? What was said? What was done?

    _____

    _____

    _____

3. What was your emotional state? To the extent possible, identify the emotions you were feeling; what you were thinking; and (if possible) the extent to which you think you were "out of control."

    _____

    _____

    _____

4. What was the other person's emotional state? To what extent would you say he or she was "out of control?"

    _____

    _____

    _____

5. How did the situation end?

    _____

    _____

    _____

6. In retrospect, what could you have done (or said) to achieve a different outcome?

    _____

    _____

    _____

7. What positive emotions (yours and/or the other person's) would have been logical replacements for any of the negative emotions involved?

    _____

    _____

    _____

B. Positive Psychology Guidelines. The following activities are associated with increasing the experience of positive emotions and emotional self-management (Peterson & others, 2001). Check the 4 or 5 that appeal most to you.

☐   1.   Stop to admire something beautiful in your surroundings once a day.

☐   2.   Do something you are fearful or anxious of doing.

☐   3.   Do something artistic every day for a week.

☐   4.   Perform an activity that strikes you as interesting although you know very little about it.

☐   5.   Give someone else credit for something.

☐   6.   When you feel annoyed with someone, even if you are justified, act graciously toward that person.

☐   7.   Increase the number of times you thank people during the day.

☐   8.   Devise a plan to accomplish a distant goal or wish.

☐   9.   Tell a funny story that makes you look silly.

☐   10.   Do something for someone else with no expectation of thanks or the favor being returned.

☐   11.   Tell someone special something you find special and good about them.

☐   12.   Deflect credit from yourself and onto someone or something else.

☐   13.   Reconsider the viewpoint of someone with whom you strongly disagree.

☐   14.   Try to act with the wisdom of the wisest person you know.

☐   15.   Make a point of focusing on how someone else feels in a situation and let him know you understand.

☐   16.   Pick something you have meant to do and do it.

Which activities would you like to include in your plans to develop emotional intelligence?

_____

_____

_____

_____

_____

"**Whatever is begun in anger, ends in shame.**"

- Benjamin Franklin

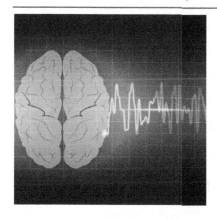

Assess Your Emotional Intelligence Competencies

"At its most basic, emotional intelligence is the ability to manage the impact of emotions on our relationships with others. It involves recognizing accurately how you and others feel at any particular time and the way emotions are affecting the situation" (Walton, 2012, p 4).

Much of Goleman's work is focused on **emotional competence,** which he defines as "learned capability based on emotional intelligence that results in outstanding performance at work" (1998, p 24). In his view, emotional intelligence determines our potential for learning the practical skills that are based in the emotional intelligence dimensions. Being high in emotional intelligence does not guarantee a person will have learned the emotional competencies that matter for work; it means only that the person has excellent *potential* to learn them.

Following are some important things to keep in mind about assessing your emotional intelligence competencies:

There are several different instruments to assess emotional intelligence, some are self-description only while others, such as the Hay Group's *Emotional and Social Competence Inventory (ESCI)*, include assessments by other people. See References for a link to this tool, which was co-developed by Goleman and Boyatzis. Our approach will rely heavily on the competencies included in the Goleman model, as illustrated and defined below:

Goleman's EI Competency Model

	PERSONAL	SOCIAL
Awareness	<u>Self-Awareness</u> • Emotional Self-Awareness • Accurate Self-Assessment • Self-Confidence	<u>Social Awareness</u> • Empathy • Organizational Awareness • Service Orientation
Actions	<u>Self-Management</u> • Emotional Self-Control • Transparency • Adaptability • Achievement • Commitment • Initiative • Optimism	<u>Relationship Management</u> • Influence • Leadership • Change Catalyst • Developing Others • Conflict Management • Teamwork & Collaboration

Self Awareness: The core of Emotional Intelligence, competencies include

- Emotional Self-Awareness: recognizing how our emotions affect our performance

- Accurate Self-Assessment: knowing one's own inner resources, abilities and limits

- Self-Confidence: a strong sense of one's self-worth and capabilities

Self Management, competencies includes

- Emotional Self-Control: keeping disruptive emotions and impulses in check

- Transparency: maintaining integrity, acting congruently with one's values

- Adaptability: flexibility in handling change

- Achievement Drive: striving to improve or meet a standard of excellence

- Commitment: aligning with group or organizational goals

- Initiative: readiness to act on opportunities

- Optimism: persistence in pursuing goals despite obstacles and setbacks

Social Awareness, competencies include

- Empathy: sensing others' feelings and perspectives; taking an active interest in their concerns

- Organizational Awareness: reading a group's emotional currents and power relationships

- Service Orientation: anticipating, recognizing and meeting customers' or clients' needs

Relationship Management, competencies include

- Influence: having impact on others

- Leadership: inspiring and guiding individuals and groups

- Change Catalyst: initiating or managing change

- Developing Others: sensing others' developmental needs and bolstering their abilities

- Conflict Management: negotiating and resolving conflict

- Teamwork and Collaboration: working with others toward a shared goal

One way to assess your EI competencies is to read the list of competencies and rate yourself on each. A simple 3-point scale – strong, weak, uncertain – is sufficient. Then give the list to someone who knows you well and ask him or her to do the same. Then compare your self-perceptions with those of the other person, noting similarities and differences. Even though the self and other perceptions may not be completely accurate, this information will be very helpful in increasing your self-awareness and focusing you on the competencies you most want to develop.

Another way is to compare your behavior against what one author calls the "Six Pillars" of emotional intelligence (Jennings, n.d.). The pillars are listed below, with some questions for you to consider as you reflect on how you measure up:

- **Self-awareness**. Simply recognizing how you feel is important. When something happens ask yourself, "How do I feel about this? Can I identify this emotion?" If you have a headache, feel rushed, or have some sense that things are not right or you are stressed, stop and identify your emotions again.

- **Empathy**. This is about being able to understand why another person feels as they do, to "put yourself in someone else's shoes." It involves listening and respecting what other people have to say and striving to understand their feelings. Ask yourself, "Why is this person saying this? What emotions is he feeling? What events or experiences led to her feeling this way?"

- **Self-regulation**. This is about not letting your emotions control you, but rather taking control of your emotions. People with good EI, "aim for assertiveness, appropriately sharing their emotions, thoughts, and beliefs with the right people at the right time as a means to let others know where they stand" (Jennings, n.d.). Ask yourself questions such as, "Am I looking at this situation honestly? What strengths do I have to help me here? What weaknesses are my emotions demonstrating?"

- **Motivation**. This is about knowing what your end goals are and keeping those in mind. It is about looking to the future, keeping your eye on what you want to achieve and not being derailed by emotions. Ask yourself, "What is my end goal? How are my emotions and behavior now helping me meet that goal?"

- **Social skills**. This is about exhibiting behaviors that help you communicate with and connect to others. It includes empathy, but also behaviors such as listening for understanding and collaborating. Ask yourself questions such as, "How are both our goals aligned? How is my behavior affecting this person? Am I being open-minded and respectful?"

- **Happiness**. EI is not focused on happiness as a result of achieving material possessions or status. Rather, it is about the happiness that results from managing positive and negative emotions in productive and satisfying ways. According to Jennings (n.d.), "Because happy people accomplish more tasks than those who are sad or depressed, it is important to note that the emotionally intelligent have the ability to control their mood to serve their purpose, motivating them to find more solutions to problems." Ask yourself, "Am I happy? Do I allow my emotions to derail my happiness? Can I have a good day even when something goes wrong? Do I let my own bad mood negatively affect my interactions with others?"

Developing Emotional Intelligence

A recent publication (Sheldon and others, 2014) reports the findings of studies examining how accurately people appraise their emotional intelligence skills. The results indicate that, at least for their professional student samples, those least skilled in emotional intelligence were largely unaware of their deficits . They also discounted as inaccurate or not relevant concrete feedback about their performance as measured on the MSCEIT (a widely used assessment of emotional intelligence). Compared with top performers, they were more reluctant to improve their emotional intelligence. **An inability to recognize either their lack of skills, or the value from improving, makes it more difficult for those who most need to improve to do so.**

The difficulties associated with developing EI competencies were also addressed by Emmerling and Goleman (2003). They contend that some development in emotional intelligence can occur through maturation and life experience, and that "the brain circuitry of emotion exhibits a fair degree of plasticity, even in adulthood. However, we argue that without sustained effort and attention individuals are unlikely to improve greatly a given aspect of their emotional intelligence (even though) there is research evidence for people's ability to improve their social and emotional competence with sustained effort and a systematic program."

Improving social-emotional competence is hard work. It requires that the person sees value in developing greater self-awareness and empathy, for example, and also is prepared for relapses as old neural pathways are extinguished and new ones are developed. Consider the following quotes:

"Capacities like empathy or flexibility differ crucially from cognitive abilities; they draw on different areas of the brain. Purely cognitive abilities are based in the neocortex, the "thinking" brain. But with personal and social competencies, additional brain areas come into play, mainly the circuitry that runs from the emotional centers —particularly the amygdala—deep in the center of the brain up to the pre-frontal lobes, the brain's executive center. Learning emotional competence retunes this circuitry."

(Goleman, 1998, p 244).

"Cognitive learning involves fitting new data and insights into existing frameworks of association and understanding, extending and enriching the corresponding neural circuitry. But emotional learning involves that and more—it requires that we also engage the neural circuitry where social and emotional habit repertoire is stored. Changing habits such as learning to approach people positively instead of avoiding them, to listen better, or to give feedback skillfully, is a more challenging task than simply adding new information to old.

Motivational factors also make social and emotional learning more difficult and complex than purely cognitive learning. Emotional learning often involves ways of thinking and acting that are more central to a person's identity. ... The prospect of learning to develop greater emotional competence is a bitter pill for many of us to swallow. It thus is much more likely to generate resistance to change."

(Cherniss & others, 1998, p 5).

What to do:		**Other actions:**	
☐	Review the list of EI competencies and give thought to how you might use them in your work.	☐	_____
		☐	_____
☐	Assess your emotional intelligence using the competencies list or "six pillars" that were introduced.	☐	_____
		☐	_____
☐	Based on the results from your EI assessment, identify competencies you will commit to developing.	☐	_____
		☐	_____

 Remember

✓ Goleman's EI Model includes both personal and social components and awareness and action dimensions. Thus, **empathy is a social awareness** competency and **adaptability is a personal action** competency.

✓ Developing emotional intelligence is more difficult than developing purely cognitive skills. You will need to be honest in examining your openness to recognizing where you need to develop, and your willingness to do the hard work of emotional learning.

 Enhance Your Learning

Watch the following 10-minute video to learn one way of assessing your emotional intelligence and seeing how it affects your levels of effectiveness and happiness:

Truly Heal. (2013). *Here is the Best EQ Test with Solution.*		Available at: https://www.youtube.com/watch?v=9VhFScF33m4

Read and complete the **Centrestar Emotional Intelligence Self-Evaluation & Development Plan** (Also included as **Appendix B**).

Centrestar. (2018). *Emotional Intelligence Self-Evaluation & Development Plan.*		Available at: https://www.centrestar.com/resources/inventories

Reinforce Your Learning

Emotional Competencies.

Spend a few minutes thinking about your emotional competencies. List those you consider strengths you can draw upon, and those where improvement might help you in working more effectively with others or responding to other workplace challenges.

Competencies I Consider Strengths	Competencies I Would Like to Improve

2. Note any ideas about what you want to do to build on your strengths or develop the competencies you would like to strengthen.

3. If you haven't yet done so, complete the Centrestar EI assessment. The website below provides a 30 statement **Centrestar Emotional Intelligence Self-Evaluation & Development Plan** which can give you additional insight into your EI competencies. Remember, self-awareness is the core of emotional intelligence (**Also included as Appendix B**).

https://www.centrestar.com/resources/inventories

Develop Your Emotional Self-Awareness

> "The first obstacle in the way of development of self-consciousness (i.e., self-awareness) in man is his conviction that he already possesses self-consciousness or, at any rate, that he can have it at any time he likes."
>
> (Ouspensky, 1954).

Emotional self-awareness is about being aware of your emotions as you are experiencing them and recognizing the potential effects that an emotion may have on your thoughts and behavior. **This is the core of emotional intelligence**. If you have emotional self-awareness, you know your values and what motivates you. You know what's most important to you, what contributes to your happiness, what your strengths and limitations are, and you are in touch with your "hot buttons." You are rarely confused by how someone else reacts to something you have said or done; you know how others perceive you. Your awareness of your own emotions and what triggers them helps you in recognizing the emotions of others.

Even though it doesn't seem like being aware of your emotions, being able to identify them as you are experiencing them, would be difficult, it can be. Sometimes, you know immediately that you are responding with anger to what someone did; at other times, you aren't sure if you're angry, surprised, or confused. And not everyone has learned to pay attention to their emotions to the point that they can begin to understand them. Without this basic level of awareness, it is impossible to use one's emotions intelligently.

One way to increase emotional self-awareness is to start paying attention to the physiological signals your body is sending when your emotions are triggered. Say, for example, one of your co-workers just criticized one of your ideas. How do you respond? If your heart is beating faster, you feel your cheeks redden, or your muscles are feeling tense, this may indicate that your immediate response is anger. Taking a moment to note your physical responses, and label the emotion, also gives you time to clarify how you are thinking. This is key to understanding why you are feeling as you do, and what you can do, if needed, to regain emotional control. With a second thought, you may conclude that you really didn't understand what your co-worker said, or that you may have over-reacted to the person's tone of voice. You may even remind yourself that you value others' input into your ideas.

Following are some important things to keep in mind as you develop your emotional self-awareness:

Goleman further describes the emotional self-awareness competencies (Goleman, 1998; CREIO newsletters).

Emotional Self-Awareness: Recognizing one's emotions and their effects. People with this competence:

- Know which emotions they are feeling and why
- Realize the links between their feelings and what they think, do and say
- Recognize how their feelings affect their performance
- Have a guiding awareness of their values and goals

Accurate Self-Assessment: Knowing one's strengths and limits. People with this competence are:

- Aware of their strengths and weaknesses and willingly learn from experience
- Open to candid feedback, new perspectives and self-development
- Able to show a sense of humor and perspective about themselves

Self-Confidence: Sureness about one's self-worth and capabilities. People with this competence:

- Present themselves with self-assurance; have "presence"
- Can voice views that are unpopular and go out on a limb for what is right
- Are decisive; make sound decisions despite uncertainties and pressures

With this set of competencies, you know:

- When you are thinking negatively
- When you are becoming angry
- How you are interpreting events
- What is really going on in the situation
- How to express accurately what you are experiencing
- How others are reacting to you
- When you are becoming defensive
- When your mood is shifting

Once you know what you are feeling and can identify the **source of those feelings**, you can begin to work on self-regulation: controlling your response to emotional stimuli.

Being mindful is key to self-awareness. Mindfulness can be defined as *moment-to-moment non-judgmental awareness*. The state of mindfulness is essentially the opposite of being on "automatic pilot." What is automatic pilot? If you're like most drivers, you have had the experience of suddenly realizing that you have travelled some distance without being aware of doing so. This generally starts a bit of worry: "Did I run a traffic light?" or "What if I had needed to avoid an accident?" In actuality, you were letting your brain do the physical driving while your conscious attention was directed elsewhere. The worries associated with this realization may be unnecessary, as it is likely that your conscious mind would have been triggered to take over when needed.

Sometimes, too, we realize that we are engaged in a conversation with someone else, or with a group of people, and have lost track of what has been said. We may have been absorbed in thinking through a problem or have drifted into fantasy land. The reality is, even though we are *there*, we are not actually *in* the present moment.

When we're on automatic pilot we are more likely to have our buttons pushed. Mindfulness gives us an opportunity to examine our first reaction and make a more intentional choice. Developing the practice of mindfulness is a powerful tool for changing emotional reactions and automatic thinking that undermine our health and well-being. It requires that we pay attention to what we are doing and specially to take note of what is working and can be built on for future strength. Mindfulness also helps us more fully experience and acknowledge the power of our positive emotions. Consider the following quote (Walton, 2012, p 27):

- "Events and situations around you can trigger old feelings and sensations which become barriers and make your mood worsen. And we can fail to notice important signals from the people we are dealing with, which suggest we had better do something differently and straight away. By becoming more aware of our thoughts, feelings and bodily sensations as they happen, we are creating the basis of greater freedom and choice in how we act and the opportunity to be more responsive to others. We don't have to go into the same habits or mental tramlines which have caused problems in the past and we can choose to act differently—perhaps building more effective relationships or coping with stresses better."

We can think in ways that help substitute positive emotions for the negative ones that may have been initially triggered.

The following can help increase emotional self-awareness:

1. Remind yourself that your actions are motivated by your feelings. Emotions put us in motion, but we can always choose our response. We are in control.

2. Make a commitment to gain a better understanding of your emotions, how they work and how you move from one to another.

3. Recognize indications of unconscious behavior – when you're on automatic pilot. Usually these are found in exaggerated reactions or inconsistencies in what you are doing and what you want to do.

4. Start labeling feelings.

5. Pay attention to your physical reactions to different negative emotions: rapid heart rate, reddening of the face, shakiness, muscular tension, perspiration.

6. Pay attention to how you think and behave when experiencing positive emotions such as joy, gratitude and affection.

7. Make time to reflect on your feelings, fears and desires.

8. Practice mindfulness techniques so you can remain in the present more often.

9. Take responsibility for your own emotions: other people do not cause you to feel bad or good: it's how you interpret and respond to what they've said or done.

Are you ready to develop your emotional self-awareness? People go through several stages of readiness before they are ready to commit to behavior change. In the first stage, they deny that they need to change or improve. They're okay, it's someone else's fault, and so on. In the second stage, they begin to see that they need to improve, but are not sure that anything can be done. So, they put off making a decision, Next, they begin to see that there are things that can be done, or learned, to bring about the change, but have not yet developed a plan for action. At fourth stage, they know they need to change, and have a plan to do so. They are now ready, committed, to change their behavior.

What to do:	Other actions:
☐ Pay attention to the thoughts and physical conditions associated with your different feelings.	☐ _____
	☐ _____
☐ After an emotionally arousing situation, think about what happened and record your responses.	☐ _____
	☐ _____
☐ Ask someone you trust to give you feedback about how you respond in emotionally charged situations.	☐ _____
	☐ _____

Remember

✓ Our actions are motivated by our emotions, but we always have the ability to choose how we will act.

✓ Ineffective emotional responses usually happen beneath our awareness. If you understand your own tendencies, you are more likely to choose a better response.

✓ People progress through degrees of readiness to make behavioral changes:

- denial of the need to change;
- uncertainty that they can;
- recognition that there is a problem, and it can be dealt with;
- creating a concrete plan to put the change into action.

It's important to know which stage you're in.

Enhance Your Learning

Watch the 11-minute summary of Ellen Langer's book, "Mindfulness," one in a series of Brian Johnson's Philosopher Notes. Consider the value of increasing your mindfulness in emotionally charged situations.

Johnson, B. (2015). *Mindfulness by Ellen Langer*.		Available at: https://www.youtube.com/watch?v=EWlhk3mr7ns&noredirect=1

Reinforce Your Learning

Increase Your Emotional Self-Awareness.

Do a quick assessment: Respond to each question by checking the frequency of your awareness.

Emotional Self-Awareness	Always/ Most of the time	Sometimes	Rarely/ Never
1. Do you recognize your emotions as they happen?			
2. Are you aware of what your thoughts are when you feel defensive?			
3. Are you aware of your negative self-talk?			
4. Are you aware of your positive self-talk?			
5. Do you know how you act when you are angry?			
6. Do you know how you act when you are defensive?			
7. Are you aware of how others perceive you?			
8. Do you avoid taking yourself too seriously?			
9. Do you know what you aspire to, what motivates you?			
10. Are you able to express your feelings and aspirations to others?			

Based on your current understanding on your level of emotional self-awareness (from the above quick assessment or other EI assessments you have completed), what do you need to work on? What ideas do you have for your next steps?

_____

_____

_____

_____

_____

_____

_____

_____

_____

_____

_____

Practice being mindful when you are in an emotionally provocative situation or realize you have been on automatic pilot. Do the following:

- ☐ Think about how you are feeling.

- ☐ Challenge your thinking: is it ideal? Potentially unrealistic?

- ☐ Think about how you want to feel.

- ☐ Identify the positive emotion associated with your preferred feeling.

- ☐ Think about how you can get there.

_____

_____

_____

_____

"The emotional brain responds to an event more quickly than the thinking brain."

- Daniel Goleman

Develop Your Skills in Emotional Regulation

> "Anyone can get angry — that is easy — but to do this to the right person, to the right extent, at the right time, with the right motive and in the right way, that is not for everyone nor is it easy."
>
> Aristotle, *Nicomachean Ethics*

Emotional regulation, or self-management is about regulating your emotions, controlling your impulsive behaviors, and modulating your reactions to create space so that more appropriate responses can be chosen. It is built on a base of strong emotional self-awareness and includes attributes such as adaptability and flexibility of thinking. For example, while a customer is yelling at you, complaining about something that was really his or her error, you do not respond impulsively – defensively or with anger. Rather, you do a quick appraisal of the situation and remind yourself that this is not personal and that your primary responsibility is to the customer. You take a deep breath (or count to 10) and respond in a polite, calm way, asking how you can make things right. You are exhibiting emotional regulation. In our work, as well as in our personal lives, it is often **necessary to control our impulses.**

Following are some important things to keep in mind as you develop your skills in emotional regulation:

Goleman's listing of the emotional self-management competencies includes a number of competencies that extend beyond emotional regulation. These competencies are definitely important to think about and are listed in the "Reinforce Your Learning" section for this concept. Our focus for this workbook must, of necessity, be narrower, so we are concentrating on the following competencies (Goleman, 1998; CREIO newsletters):

Self-Management/Regulation

Emotional Self-Control: Managing disruptive emotions and impulses. People with this competence:

- Manage their impulsive feelings and distressing emotions well
- Stay composed, positive and unflappable even in trying moments
- Think clearly and stay focused under pressure

Adaptability: Flexibility in handling change and being comfortable with and open to novel ideas and new information. People with this competence:

- Smoothly handle multiple demands, shifting priorities and rapid change
- Adapt their responses and tactics to fit fluid circumstances
- Are flexible in how they see events
- Seek out fresh ideas from a wide variety of sources; generate new ideas
- Entertain original solutions to problems; take fresh perspectives

Optimism: Persistence in pursuing goals despite obstacles and setbacks. People with this competence:

- Persist in seeking goals despite obstacles and setbacks
- Operate from hope of success rather than fear of failure
- See setbacks as due to manageable circumstances, not as personal flaws

With this set of competencies, you can:

- Keep your impulses under control
- Calm yourself quickly when angry
- Quickly switch from negative to positive thinking
- Relax in pressure situations
- Act productively in anxiety-arousing or high change situations
- Reflect on negative feelings without being distressed
- Stay calm when you are the target of anger from others
- Stay hopeful and optimistic in the face of disappointment, setbacks or obstacles
- Keep open for new ideas, fresh perspectives and deeper insight

Self-management includes a strong element of personal responsibility. You manage your attitudes and behaviors so that you responsibly meet your obligations to your work and to other institutions and people. It also means that you take responsibility for setting and working toward professional and personal goals and for managing yourself toward a happy, fulfilled life. Being able to regulate your emotions, so that you control them rather than them controlling you, is fundamental to self-management.

Most of us develop some level of self-management as children. We complete our chores (without too much complaining), we do our homework, we go to school and attend family functions. The older we get the more self-management is expected of us. But not everyone meets these responsibilities to the same degree, and what we do and do not manage depends very heavily on our life experiences, personal values and emotional intelligence. How effective is your self-management? Consider questions such as:

- Do I cause myself problems by not being proactive? For example, do I frequently pay bills or taxes late, and therefore incur penalties? Do I put off maintenance on my car or home?

- Do I know what my own goals are: current job, career, personal life?

- Have I thought through the steps I need to take to realize these goals? Do I take steps to achieve these goals every day?

- Do I take responsibility to get thing done without other people having to remind or "nag" me to do it?

- Do I procrastinate on getting important things done?

- Am I able to handle difficult situations and disappointments positively and optimistically?

- Do I meet change willingly and proactively?

- Do I handle emotionally strained interactions with care and confidence?

- Do I take responsibility for the after-effects of my inappropriate responses rather than blaming other people or things?

As we saw in concept 5, emotional self-awareness involves taking the time to think about your emotions, your reactions, and your action choices. Self-management takes it a step further. As one psychologist puts it, "In the context of Emotional Intelligence, self-management refers to the methods, skills, and strategies by which individuals can effectively manage their bodies, thoughts, feelings, and behaviors in a way that is consistent with the achievement of their objectives" (Spradling, n.d.). She recommends some ways that we can **improve self-management in four areas**:

- *Management of your body*: This is about keeping yourself healthy, eating the right foods, getting enough sleep, exercising, and so forth.

- *Management of your thoughts*: An unfocused mind can wander to thoughts that are stressful, that produce unnecessary worry, anxiety and confusion. Learn to calm your mind. For some people, meditation works; for others, concentrating on a specific activity such as a sport, a movie, playing with their kids, listening to music or reading a good book. Think of this as needing an escape, every day, to focus on something that you enjoy and find relaxing.

- *Management of your feelings*: Negative emotions can be difficult to tame once they are fully expressed. Early recognition that an emotion is building and paying attention to what you are thinking can help keep negative emotions under control. You can also try to change your life to avoid situations that add to your stress without adding value.

- *Management of your behavior*: In the workplace managing your behavior may be the most important aspect of self-management. It is important to remember that behavior results from your emotions, largely based on your appraisal of the situation. If you manage your body, thoughts, and feelings, then managing your behaviors will be easier. Some tricks you can use to help are taking a time-out when you need to get your thoughts or emotions in order, refusing to answer any questions or talk when you are angry, and working to develop empathy and better understand your co-workers.

Putting together some self-awareness and self-management concepts, the following **tips** to build personal EI competencies are very helpful and fairly easy to follow (Crompton, 2010):

- *Keep a "trigger" journal*. If you find controlling your emotions difficult, keep a journal of events and interactions that trigger your negative emotions. Then, look at the common issues that are your triggers and look for specific ways to manage your emotions in these types of situations.

- *Pay attention to your "self-talk"*. We all have a little voice inside us that says, "Well that is just stupid," or "I can't do that." Pay attention to what your voice is telling you, and when you hear it being negative, turn it around. Work on stopping negative self-talk and turning it into positive talk.

- *Always remember that you choose your behavior*. Take responsibility. In every situation you have the option to make it worse by giving in to your anger, frustration or despair,, or to not let your emotions get the better of you.

"The ability to control impulses, or more specifically to control the desire to act on them, is primarily about deferred gratification. Being impulsive creates problems in relationships and limits the rational thinking needed to deal with others" (Walton, 2012, p 55). Being able to control impulses involves being aware of the situation you are in and evaluating the possible consequences of your behavior. If you act impulsively (e.g., yell back at the customer "It's your fault,") you will realize immediate gratification: the customer was both rude and wrong and doesn't have the right to speak to you that way. So, you're giving him what he deserves. If instead, you find a way to focus on something other than your emotional state, you won't have immediate gratification but likely will have behaved in a way more suitable for the time and place. Taking a few seconds allows the "stressor" hormones to dissipate and increases your ability to think more clearly.

Situations can appear impossible when their implications are unknown. When you can evaluate and face them, you can exert control over the amygdala's signals that you are in danger or at risk. Your choice, for example, to focus on counting to ten rather than on your anger, will inhibit the amygdala's activity. Your anger will reduce, and you are likely to behave more thoughtfully and tactfully if the anger resulted from an interaction with another person, or in a more productive way if the anger was generated by an equipment problem.

As introduced previously, mindfulness is an excellent way to widen the gap between impulse and action. These techniques help you take the time to make a better choice about how to respond. Consider the following:

- To manage negative emotions, ask: why does it bother me? What are my beliefs? Are some of my beliefs dysfunctional to me? What are my needs? How can I act to meet them?

- When negative emotions begin to stir, distance yourself. Even a brief distance in time or space can help you choose your response.

- Breathe deeply. This sends more oxygen to your brain and helps dissipate the stress hormones.

- Label the emotion or emotions you are feeling.

- Do a reality check: what is really going on in this situation? Separate the truth (reality) from the fiction (distorted perception).

- Assess the magnitude of the situation: how important will this be next week or next year?

- Consciously use positive self-talk, and positive other-talk (e.g., he is not the enemy, they are not trying to humiliate me, she is pretty reasonable, she must be stressed, etc.)

- Find something in the situation that is positive or offers hope or learning.

What to do:	Other actions:
☐ Recognize where you need to manage your impulsive behavior and decide how you will do so.	☐ _____ ☐ _____
☐ Make a commitment to increase your self-management, in whatever area (i.e., body, thoughts, feelings, behavior) you consider most significant to your present situation.	☐ _____ ☐ _____ ☐ _____
☐ Work on replacing negative self-talk (and negative other-talk) with positive.	☐ _____

 **Remember**

✓ Your emotions have significant impact on your thoughts and actions. When your emotions—especially negative ones—are strong, you need to step back, slow down and think before acting.

✓ The three competency areas for self-management are: emotional self-control, adaptability and optimism. In combination, they equip us to handle difficult interactions, respond to disrupted expectations, and meet the demands of change with positive expectations.

 Enhance Your Learning

Watch the 11-minute summary of the book, *"The Emotional Life of Your Brain"* by Davidson and Begley, one in a series of Brian Johnson's Philosopher Notes. Consider how you can apply these concepts to your development of emotional self-management.

Johnson, B. (2015). *"The Emotional Life of Your Brain"*, Davidson and Begley.		Available at: https://www.youtube.com/watch?v=Z2ptg8ZK9Ek

Reinforce Your Learning

A. **Work on Your Mindfulness**. The following four-step process will help you move away from operating on "automatic." It does require some practice but is very helpful when you need to shift away from one of the negative emotions, such as irritation, impatience, anxiety or anger (Fralich, 2005).

Step 1: **Stop**

- Bring your awareness to the negative emotion as soon as possible.

- Begin to recognize the early warning signals of the emotional reaction.

- Remind yourself: "I need to pay attention to this—now."

Step 2: **Breathe**

- Become sensitive to the natural softening quality of breath.

- Use body-mind communication: send a mental message to release and let go.

- Relaxing into the exhale, allow the negative emotion to soften.

Step 3: **Reflect**

- Appraise the situation: What is my old pattern here?

- Is my reaction supported by old myths or messages?

- What part of my reaction is flowing in from past experiences?

- What resources and options do I have right here in the present moment?

- Can I change my mind about how I see myself in this situation?

- What is my best insight about this situation? What do I want to remember?

Step 4: **Choose**

- Having become more aware of my reaction, settled myself a bit and tapped into my insight, what is possible here?

- What is effective or skillful?

- Can I shift my old pattern and make a creative choice?

- What is my best choice under all the circumstances?

B. **Plan to Work Through a Difficult Situation**. Complete the following activity to help you prepare yourself, in advance, to handle a difficult interaction with another person.

1. Describe an upcoming situation (on ongoing interaction) that you expect to result in anger or other strong emotion—on your, or the other person's, part.

2. How have you responded in past interactions with this individual (or over this issue)— emotionally and behaviorally?

3. If the result, was you became angry, frustrated, overly anxious, or felt humiliated or depressed, what "automatic thoughts" provoked the negative emotional response?

4. How did you express your emotion? What did you do?

5. What assumptions have you made about the other person's character or motives? Do you need to conceptualize him or her in a more positive or neutral light?

6. What will you do to gain control so that you either do not "automatically" respond with a negative emotion or, if you do, you express it in a productive way?

7. What should you be telling yourself before, during and after the interaction that represent realistic, rational statements?

C. **Review the competencies in Goleman's Model** (below) and see if you want to add development in any of these to your plans for developing your emotional intelligence.

Self- Management/Regulation

Emotional Self-Control: Managing disruptive emotions and impulses. People with this competence:

❑ Manage their impulsive feelings and distressing emotions well

❑ Stay composed, positive and unflappable even in trying moments

❑ Think clearly and stay focused under pressure

Transparency: Maintaining standards of honesty and integrity; taking responsibility for personal performance. People with this competence:

❑ Act ethically and are above reproach

❑ Build trust through their reliability and authenticity

❑ Admit their own mistakes and confront unethical actions in others

❑ Take tough, principled stands even if they are unpopular

❑ Meet commitments and keep promises; hold themselves accountable

❑ Are organized and careful in their work

Adaptability: Flexibility in handling change and being comfortable with and open to novel ideas and new information. People with this competence:

❑ Smoothly handle multiple demands, shifting priorities and rapid change

❑ Adapt their responses and tactics to fit fluid circumstances

❑ Are flexible in how they see events

❑ Seek out fresh ideas from a wide variety of sources; generate new ideas

❑ Entertain original solutions to problems; take fresh perspectives

Achievement Drive: Striving to improve or meet a standard of excellence. People with this competence:

❑ Are results-oriented; high drive to meet their objectives and standards

❑ Set challenging goals and take calculated risks

❑ Pursue information to reduce uncertainty and find ways to do better

❑ Learn how to improve their performance

Commitment: Aligning with the goals of the group or organization. People with this competence:

❑ Readily make personal or group sacrifices to meet an organizational goal

❑ Find a sense of purpose in the larger mission

❑ Use the group's core values in making decisions and clarifying choices

❑ Actively seek out opportunities to fulfill the group's mission

Initiative: Readiness to act on opportunities. People with this competence:

❑ Are ready to seize opportunities

❑ Pursue goals beyond what's required or expected of them

❑ Cut through red tape; bend the rules when necessary to get the job done

❑ Mobilize others through unusual, enterprising efforts

Optimism: Persistence in pursuing goals despite obstacles and setbacks. People with this competence:

❑ Persist in seeking goals despite obstacles and setbacks

❑ Operate from hope of success rather than fear of failure

❑ See setbacks as due to manageable circumstances, not as personal flaws

Read Other People's Emotions Effectively

Just as being aware of your own emotions is the basic ingredient of personal competence, reading the emotions of others is basic to social competence. The social competencies are very important aspects of emotional intelligence. Often referred to as *social intelligence*, these competencies enable people to understand and make connections with other people and to forge positive, productive work relationships. They are essential for anyone who aspires to a leadership position within virtually any organization.

In Goleman's model, the ability to read the emotions of other people is part of social awareness, with the foundational competency being empathy:

> **Empathy**: Sensing others' feelings and perspective and taking an active interest in their concerns. People with this competence:

- Are attentive to emotional cues and listen well

- Show sensitivity and understand others' perspectives

- Help out based on understanding other people's needs and feelings

The other competencies under social awareness are **organizational awareness and service orientation**. The full list is shown in the "Reinforce Your Learning" section for this concept, and some of these competencies are discussed in Key Concepts 8 and 9.

Following are some important things to keep in mind about reading others' emotions:

To read other people's emotions requires that you focus your attention on them rather than on yourself. Your awareness of your own emotions and how you display them will help you recognize another person's emotions, but empathy involves getting beyond yourself into the other person's perspective. **The essence of empathy is sensing what others feel when they have not expressed their feelings verbally.** Empathy is essential for success in any job where performance depends on working effectively with others.

Emotions are most often conveyed nonverbally: through facial expression, body language, tone of voice, rate of speaking and the like. While not everyone expresses the same emotion in exactly the same way, it is often possible to recognize both that another person is experiencing a significant emotion and what that emotion is. With that recognition you can shift your thinking to figuring out how the other person is thinking and to understanding what may have triggered that emotion. You are then in a position to choose a response that conveys your understanding. The better you know the other person, the easier and more accurate this recognition, understanding and responding become.

Your ability to empathize is based on your personal competencies of emotional self-awareness and self-management. If you cannot sense your own feelings or regulate them, you will not be able to tune into what someone else is feeling and think through how to respond.

Whenever you are interacting with another person, it is important to pay attention to the *how* as well as the *what* of the other person's messages. Listen to the voice: tone, pitch, loudness, rate, and rhythm. Pay attention to the face: eye contact and facial expressions. Pay attention to body language: gestures, posture, sitting or standing, movement, distance and touch. Listen actively: that is, reflect back what you are hearing, ask questions that help you get clarification, and acknowledge what the other person is saying. This type of intentional awareness helps keep your focus on understanding the other person. As mentioned earlier, this understanding will help guide your choice of response.

To express empathy, you also need to be mindful of the *how* of your messages: are your voice, facial expressions and body language conveying that you are paying attention, listening, encouraging, supporting and being understanding? Do your words and the nonverbal elements of your message match?

Being empathetic requires excellent listening skills and a value placed on listening for understanding. While an empathic response may well include sharing a similar experience or suggesting an action for the other person to consider, your first obligation is to subordinate your need to speak to your need to understand.

People who do not listen, either because of lack of skills or lack of desire, come across as uncaring, disinterested or indifferent. When we sense that someone is not listening to us, we tend to talk less or stop talking altogether. You can **choose not to listen** as an emotional self-regulator in certain situations, when this is a consciously chosen response. If it is not a conscious choice, or becomes habitual, it seriously limits your ability to understand others.

Have you ever noticed that when two people are engaged in conversation their postures, rate of speaking and facial expressions tend to match even though they may have been different when they first started to talk. This alignment seems a natural response, below full conscious awareness, and operates to establish similar emotional states: whether positive or negative. Part of social intelligence is recognizing this tendency and knowing when to choose nonverbal messages to help create a different emotional climate.

Our brains are actually pre-wired to pick up the emotions of others. **Mirror neurons,** thought to be part of our natural "survival kit," are activated when we are exposed to another person's emotions and basically tell us that we ought to be feeling the same way. When we consciously or unconsciously detect someone else's emotions our mirror neurons reproduce those emotions, creating a sense of shared experience.

The ability to read the emotions of others and to empathize with them helps create connections and builds trust. Some other important results include the following (Akers & Porter, 2016):

- When you better **understand the signals** that others are sending, you are better able to respond to them.

- Empathy helps you take on a **service orientation**, anticipating the needs of others and striving to understand them.

- If you're in a leadership position, empathy can help you better understand how to **develop skills** in the people you supervise.

- Empathy helps you to **understand diverse groups** and **cultures.**

- Empathy helps you to develop the necessary social skills to be a **more effective individual** including influence and negotiation, communication, leadership, problem solving and conflict management, building relationships and teams, and collaboration and cooperation.

There is a difference between *empathy* and *sympathy.* Essentially, **sympathy** is a reflection of how you feel in response to someone else's situation or experience. You are sorry that the person is going through what they are and expressing sympathy can be very caring and helpful to the other person. **Empathy** is the ability to understand **the other person's feelings and view of things**, to put yourself in the other person's situation and feel, at least a bit, what he or she is feeling.

What to do:	Other actions:
☐ Pay attention to how people are acting when they speak: voice, facial expression, body language.	☐ _____ ☐ _____
☐ Get beyond your own emotions and tune in to what someone else is feeling.	☐ _____ ☐ _____
☐ Observe people as they are talking together, looking for visible cues about their emotional states.	☐ _____ ☐ _____

Remember

✓ To read other people's emotions requires that you focus your attention on them rather than on yourself.

✓ Emotions are most often conveyed nonverbally: through facial expression, body language, tone of voice, rate of speaking and the like.

✓ Sympathy is feeling sorry for someone; it does not mean that you have to understand them. Empathy is understanding what the person is experiencing and why.

Enhance Your Learning

Watch the following 16-minute Ted Talk about empathy:

TEDx. (2015). *Reimaging Empathy: The Transformative Nature of Empathy*.		Available at: https://www.youtube.com/watch?v=e4aHb_GTRVo

Watch the following 1-minute video about empathy:

SurePeople. (2015). *The Importance of Empathy in Leadership*.		Available at: https://www.youtube.com/watch?v=RQoNnleoKG4

Reinforce Your Learning

A. **Listening with empathy.** Check the degree to which you engage in the behavior for each of the following questions. Review your responses and select one or two of the aspects you would like to improve and note your initial ideas for how to do so.

	Mostly/ Always	Sometimes	Rarely/ Never
1. Do you control your urge to let your mind wander to other concerns or problems while you are listening to another person?			
2. Can you successfully block out or manage miscellaneous distractions while listening to another?			
3. Do you recognize when you are beginning to fake attention, and quickly reengage?			
4. If you missed something another person said (because of temporary inattention) are you able to apologize and ask him or her to repeat?			
5. Are you able to maintain eye contact with the person with whom you are talking?			
6. Are you aware of your nonverbal communication tendencies when talking with another person?			
7. Are you aware of your nonverbal communication tendencies when talking with a group?			
8. Are you able to attend to the nonverbal cues given by the person to whom you are speaking?			
9. Are you able to attend to the nonverbal cues given by different members of a group while interacting with them?			

	Mostly/ Always	Sometimes	Rarely/ Never
10. When others express emotions, are you able to respond in appropriate ways (respectful, sensitive, caring, etc.)?			
11. Are you able to regulate your emotions, so that you do not react impulsively to the other person's expressions?			
12. Does your posture communicate interest and openness to the other person's message?			
13. Are you able to follow, with understanding, what the other person is saying, both verbally and nonverbally?			
14. Are you able to use silence as a method to keep the other person giving you more information?			
15. Are you able to convey acknowledgement of what the other person is saying?			
16. Are you able to interject, to reflect back or clarify the other person's message, without taking over the conversation?			
17. Are you the type of person that others seek out because you are able to listen and empathize?			

B. **Social Awareness Competencies**. The competencies included in Goleman's model are listed below. You might want to review these, to see if there are any that you want to consider more closely as you plan to develop your emotional intelligence.

Social Awareness

Empathy: Sensing others' feelings and perspective and taking an active interest in their concerns. People with this competence:

❑ Are attentive to emotional cues and listen well

❑ Show sensitivity and understand others' perspectives

❑ Help out based on understanding other people's needs and feelings

Organizational Awareness: Reading a group's emotional currents and power relationships. People with this competence:

❑ Accurately read key power relationships

❑ Detect crucial social networks

❑ Understand forces that shape views and actions of clients and customers

❑ Accurately read situations and internal and external organizational realities

Service Orientation: Anticipating, recognizing and meeting customers' needs. People with this competence:

❑ Understand customers' needs and match them to services or products

❑ Seek ways to increase customers' satisfaction and loyalty

❑ Gladly offer appropriate assistance

❑ Grasp a customer's perspective, acting as a trusted advisor

"When anger rises, think of the consequences."

- Confucius

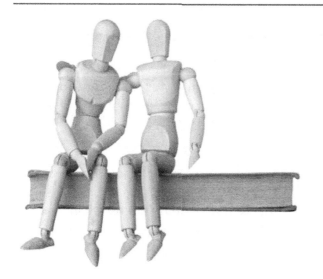

Support Others in Managing Their Emotions

With a good understanding of another person's perspective and emotions, we can sometimes help them to better understand and manage their own emotions. As we saw in Key Concept Seven, our brains have been equipped with mirror neurons designed to mimic what another person is doing or feeling. There is even a special subset of mirror neurons to detect laughter and smiles! Mirror neurons are highly important in situations where people are interacting to solve problems, make decisions, negotiate agreements and collaborate in reaching a challenging, common goal. Realizing that your emotional state will affect the feelings of those around you increases your responsibility for emotional self-regulation—especially for doing what you can to experience more positive emotions more of the time. Why – because we think better, more creatively, and more openly when experiencing positive emotions.

With this set of skills, you are able to:

- Accurately reflect back to others the feelings they are experiencing,

- Help others recognize and label their emotions,

- Spot when another person's emotions are making things difficult,

- Give feedback to others about what you've observed in their behavior in ways that do not provoke defensiveness,

- Use body language to signal positive emotions,

- Defuse situations where negative emotions are building,

- Manage group emotions,

- Be seen as approachable by others, and

- Avoid provoking unnecessary negative emotions by helping others meet some basic needs.

Following are some important things to keep in mind about helping others manage their emotions:

The ability to express yourself clearly and respectfully is important in most jobs and job situations, but it is critical when your goal is to help others manage their emotions. At a basic level, this includes:

- Being appropriately friendly,

- Expressing interest in the thoughts and experiences of others,

- Using facial expressions and body language consistent with being interested in, and open to, the ideas of others,

- Choosing non-offensive words that are at the right level of difficulty, and

- Speaking at a rate and volume that make it easy for people to follow.

When you are trying to gain control of a situation, persuade others to do something they prefer not to do, or de-escalate a conflict, helping people manage their emotions requires more than the basics. The following suggestions apply whether interacting with one person or a group:

- Speak in a calm, quiet voice at a pace slightly slower than usual.

- Gain agreement on small points before moving to the bigger issues to build a collaborative climate.

- Plan on stating what you want or expect more than once, especially if emotions are strong.

- Have one or two ways to keep your emotions from interfering with your preferred results: how can you "keep your cool?" Consider, for example: rational, positive self-talk, a mental device to distance yourself, and focusing on the results you want.

- Listen actively, acknowledging what is said and paraphrasing or restating the positions of others in positive ways.

- Do not interrupt or argue.

For any interaction, remember the concept of **mirroring.** Use your facial expressions and body language to project the emotions you want the others to experience. **Avoid mirroring behaviors that reflect negative emotions**. For example, assume you are in a heated debate with a co-worker. Both of you are standing, speaking quite loudly, pointing at each other and exhibiting other signs of anger. If you pause a moment, take a deep breath, sit down, and begin to talk in a more moderate voice, chances are the other person will mirror your behavior – or at least stop the build-up of anger. Rather than a debate, your interaction will become a conversation and you can move forward more positively.

Core concerns. Sometimes, the best way to help another person manage his or her emotions is to prevent or minimize the eruption of negative emotions. The work of Fisher and Shapiro (2005) focused on emotions involved in negotiation situations, but their work has applications for other interpersonal interactions as well. They identify five human needs, or core concerns, that trigger positive or negative emotions to the extent that they are met during an interaction. Being aware of these concerns can help you understand why people react as they do and also act as a guide for stimulating positive emotions in you and the other person. The core concerns and how they are met are described below (Fisher & Shapiro, 2005, p. 17):

- **Appreciation**: When you show appreciation, you acknowledge the other person's ideas, feelings and behaviors as having merit. When these are devalued or ignored, predictable emotions are anger, disgust and repulsion. These emotions push the individual to react negatively, even when contrary to his or her best interests.

- **Affiliation:** When you treat the other person as a colleague, this need is met. If you treat the other person as an adversary or keep him or her at a distance, he or she is likely to disengage, to move away rather than toward you or what you want.

- **Autonomy:** When you respect the other person's freedom to decide important matters, this need is met. It is unmet if this freedom is impinged upon or denied. Predictable emotions associated with denial of autonomy are guilt, shame and spitefulness, all of which can lead to rigid thinking.

- **Status:** When you acknowledge the other person's position, experience, or standing in the group or organization, you meet this need. If you do not treat the other person respectfully, or worse, treat the other person as inferior, he or she may feel anxious, regretful or sad. In response, he or she may be deceitful or fail to honor agreements.

- **Role:** When the tasks and responsibilities of the other person are defined so as to be meaningful and fulfilling, this need is met. If these are limited, not personally fulfilling, or trivialized, the emotional response may be envy or jealousy.

When the core concerns are met, common emotions include enthusiasm, affection, happiness, pride, hopefulness and a feeling of relief or relaxation. These emotions lead to behaviors that are more cooperative, collaborative, creative, and trustworthy. Thus, helping others manage their emotions often requires your taking actions to ensure that the individual's core concerns are met reasonably, and within parameters appropriate for the situation.

How you communicate is critical to your ability to help others manage their emotions. When you are effective, you are able to listen to and truly understand other people. You are able to anticipate, or at least recognize, their concerns, goals and needs. You can use that information to decide how best to present your own concerns, goals and needs, thus working toward more positive, productive and relationship-building interactions.

As we've mentioned previously, another person's emotional reactions are often based less on **what** was said and more on **how** it was said. Framing your words properly is important. Consider this scenario:

- Bridget approaches her supervisor Mike and says, "My father is in the hospital, and I have to take a few days off to be with him." Mike remains seated, sighs in annoyance, and says, with obvious exasperation, "I'm really sorry that your dad is sick, but you know we need to get this project done." He pauses, obviously rattled as Bridget just stands, silent. Mike continues, with annoyance in his voice, "Who do you suggest I get to finish the work while you are away?" **At this point, what emotions do you think Bridget is experiencing? What emotions do you think Mike is experiencing?**

- What if this happens, instead? Bridget says to Mike, "My father is in the hospital, and I have to take a few days off to be with him." Mike gives her direct eye contact, then stands up and walks closer to Bridget with a relaxed posture and sincere expression and says, "I'm really sorry that your dad is sick. Of course, you want to be with him." Mike pauses, then says with a pained expression, "I'm really sorry, but I have to ask… you know we need to get this project done." He pauses, obviously unhappy that he has to bring this up during such a difficult time, "Can you suggest who I can ask to finish the work while you are away?" **At this point, what emotions do you think Bridget is experiencing? What about Mike's emotions? Did Mike's response help Bridget manage her emotions?**

Helping others manage their emotions is important, and, although some of the suggestions seem to be common sense, they are not always easy to follow. It will help if the following become your daily, standard practice:

- *Keep a good attitude*. If your attitude is generally good – positive, optimistic – people will enjoy being around you and are more likely to share information with you and listen to you. Being positive also helps you to keep your emotions in check and your stress levels manageable.

- *Remember The Golden Rule*. Treat people the way that you would like to be treated.

- *Listen*. Too often people sit in a conversation simply waiting for their turn to speak, when instead they should be listening. Take the time to listen to other people. **Hear** their **words**, read their **body language** and **tune in to their emotions**. If you find that you often misunderstand people, try repeating back to them what they have said to ensure that you understood correctly.

- *Be open minded*. Be willing to change your views in the face of new evidence.

- *Show genuine interest in others*. Rather than faking interest, which is usually obvious to the other person, **look for commonalities**, for areas that you can discuss that truly interest you, and make only honest, authentic comments.

- *Think before you speak*. An important part of emotional intelligence is the ability to take time to think through your words. This is especially true when you are involved with helping others manage their emotions. If you speak in haste, or respond impulsively with defensiveness or aggressiveness, you will fuel misunderstanding and distance yourself from the other person. Be okay with silence; many masters at getting people to talk, such as police detectives, **use silence to their advantage.** They know that most people are uncomfortable with silence and will often share information just to fill the air with sound.

- Communicate with actions, not just words. Be aware of your body language and practice reading other people's body language.

What to do:	Other actions:	
☐ Consider the effects of mirroring on the climate and use body language to signal positive emotions.	☐ _____	
	☐ _____	
☐ Help others manage their emotions by acting to ensure that their core concerns are met reasonably.	☐ _____	
	☐ _____	
☐ When you are trying to gain control of a situation, have ways to stay positive and keep your cool.	☐ _____	
	☐ _____	

Remember

✓ The ability to think before you speak is an important part of emotional intelligence, especially when you are involved in helping others manage their emotions.

✓ An important part of helping others manage their emotions is giving them feedback about your observations in ways that do not provoke defensiveness.

✓ Meeting our co-workers' needs for appreciation, affiliation, and autonomy help them experience more positive emotions.

Enhance Your Learning

Watch the following 3-minute video to learn more about the impact of emotional intelligence on career success, and consider how you can apply this information in your work:

ExpertAcademy. (2013). *Emotional Intelligence for Career Success*.		Available at: https://www.youtube.com/watch?v=Cj3QsDSVWDo

If you are Interested in learning more about body language, check out the book, *What Every Body Is Saying*, by Joe Navarro.

Reinforce Your Learning

How well do you do in reading and helping others manage their emotions? Respond to the following questions.

1. Think about your experience in interacting with different people. Can you identify people whose emotions you find easy to read? What about people whose emotions you find difficult to read? What do you think accounts for this difference? Consider how well you know them and similarities or differences in: jobs or organizational positions; educational or previous work experience; age, gender or race; types of situations in which you interact.

_____

_____

_____

_____

_____

_____

_____

_____

_____

2. Reflect on a situation where you helped another person manage his or her emotions. What was the situation? What emotions were involved? What did you do that helped? Could you have done more?

3. Reflect on a situation where you could have helped another person manage his or her emotions but did not do so. Why not?

4. What will you do to increase the positive impact you have through helping others manage their emotions?

"All learning has an emotional base."

– Plato

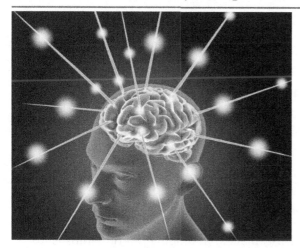

Identify Essential Social Intelligence Competencies

Social intelligence competencies include both **social awareness** and **relationship management**. As well as understanding the needs and motivations of others, a socially intelligent individual is able to make connections with associates, gain their trust and provide support and encouragement to help them develop and succeed.

An important part of social intelligence is **organizational awareness**: understanding the realities that affect the organization, being in tune with the culture, and being politically astute. Socially intelligent people do not make political blunders; they know how to get results within the context of the organization's norms and values. They are aware of both the formal and informal structures and know whose support they need in order to achieve what needs to be done. They do not use their organizational knowledge for their own aggrandizement, but rather to achieve positive outcomes for the organization and its members and customers.

Goleman's (1998) **relationship management** competencies include:

- Influence,
- Leadership,
- Change Catalyst,
- Developing Others,
- Conflict Management, and
- Teamwork and Collaboration.

A more detailed description of his model is provided in the "Reinforce Your Learning" section for this concept. While a lot of the studies examining the impact of these competencies on career success and organizational performance have focused on executives and other people in leadership positions, it is difficult to imagine many jobs in today's organizations where such skills are not needed.

Following are some important things to keep in mind as you consider social intelligence competencies:

Anyone wishing to develop skills in the relationship management competencies needs to commit to learning some of the basic principles and best practices associated with, for example, leadership and building teams. They also need opportunities to apply what they have learned in different situations, practicing and honing their skills and confidence over time. Understandably, this type of learning is beyond the scope of this course. What we focus on is providing some general guidelines for managing relationships and reviewing the behaviors typical of emotionally intelligent people.

In today's interconnected, complex and dynamic workplaces, managing relationships is perhaps more important, and more challenging than ever before. Most of us need to manage multiple work relationships: with teammates, managers, colleagues in other departments, customers, suppliers, contractors and regulators. We also have personal relationships: family members, friends, neighbors, and service providers. How you **manage relationships directly affects** your performance and satisfaction at work, and your overall **happiness in life.**

Always work to build effective relationships. **Networking** may have become a buzzword, but for good reason – relationships with other people make things happen. You never know when you will need information or some type of assistance from someone, so always work to build relationships and keep connections intact.

Be present. When communicating with another person—to provide direction (leadership) or to give feedback to help them develop skills—be mentally present. Pay attention to what you are saying, and hearing, and be on the alert for signs of your or the other person's emotional reactions. When you are communicating to strengthen a team, look for signs of buy-in or resistance and reflect back or ask questions to surface possible issues for discussion. Scan for evidence of real engagement as opposed to superficial commitment. Know when someone other than you needs to speak. Recognize those times when someone else can have more positive influence on the team than you can.

Know that emotional self-awareness and self-management affect your ability to reach others:

- When you understand your own emotions, you can avoid common pitfalls such as making rushed, impulsive decisions. You are aware of how your behavior affects others. You are also better able to pick up what others are feeling and take that into consideration in choosing what to do or say.

- Practicing self-management helps you to set goals, commit to attaining them, and keep your emotions from interfering with an outcome you prefer. You are also acting as a role model for others, gaining their trust and their willingness to support you and to learn from you.

Some other guidelines for managing relationships include:

- **Manage your health and stress level**. When we are stressed out, tired, or otherwise not at our physical and emotional best, managing relationships becomes more difficult. If you are experiencing these conditions, it may be wise to put off resolving a conflict or giving someone performance feedback until you are feeling better.

- **Work together**. Be a caring person and learn to see things from the other person's point of view – practice empathy.

- **Learn to give up without a sense of losing.** Remember that giving in to another person— whether it is acknowledging that you were wrong, changing your opinion, or just letting the other person prevail— is not a failure. Reasonable people need to cooperate and to compromise. When a situation becomes a battle of wills where everyone refuses to compromise little good results.

- **Be willing to self-disclose.** Share information about yourself to help others get to know you better. It is difficult to build trust with people who don't reveal much about their feelings or aspirations. On the other hand, disclosing information that is too personal, unrelated to the task, or negative about other people can cause problems with trust.

- **Work on being open-minded.** Do not immediately reject an idea that is different from yours. Ask for ideas from others regularly and demonstrate that you listen to and value their ideas. Take the view that there are many different ways to solve a problem and that "doing things the same old way" is not always the best choice.

- **Always be respectful**. Even when you are interacting with people who exhibit difficult behavior, you owe them respect. Do not attack them with accusatory or judgmental statements. Have an exit strategy, if you need one, but make sure it is not inflammatory or hurtful.

- **Support others**. Focus on the strengths of others and reinforce their positive aspects rather than focusing on the negatives. Acknowledge their achievements and show appreciation for their contributions. Provide encouragement and support when it is needed.

- **Know what you can and cannot control**. Accept what you can affect or influence and deal only with that. You do not have full control over the quality of your relationships; there are others involved who have equivalent influence. And there are often other issues and complexities of which you are unaware that are in play. You *can* control your emotional response, and that is significant.

- **Approach interpersonal conflict with a win-win attitude.** Understand that interpersonal conflict is a natural and inevitable feature of people working together. The answer is not to suppress or avoid conflict, but rather to recognize it early, identify its causes, and work for fair resolutions that meet the needs of all parties. It is not about finding who is "right" or who is "wrong," or about getting caught in the past. It's about what's best for the team or organization and how do we get there.

Walton (2012, p 88) lists some emotionally intelligent relationship management behaviors. A person with these competencies:

- Actively seeks ways of resolving conflict

- Is skilled at winning people over

- Demonstrates empathy with others' feelings

- Enables others to trust and confide in him or her

- Respects and relates well to others from varying backgrounds

- Challenges bias and intolerance

- Accurately reads key power relationships

- Understands the forces that shape others' views

- Uses a win-win approach

- Fosters open communication

> "The basis of interpersonal influence is not simply the power of your personality or fluency. It lies in the strength of the relationships and social bonds which exist, whether in a team, organization or community. Those relationships stem from what you are doing and how you communicate during the time you spend together. Much of that is defined by your role, and how much emphasis you place on task or people in your conversation."
>
> (Walton, 2012, p 77)

What to do:

- ☐ Recognize the importance of social intelligence, especially managing work relationships.

- ☐ Review the guidelines for managing work relationships and identify 1 or 2 that you will begin following.

- ☐ Choose one interaction where you will focus on being present throughout the interaction.

Other actions:

- ☐ _____

- ☐ _____

- ☐ _____

- ☐ _____

- ☐ _____

- ☐ _____

Remember

✓ Leaders, whether formal or informal, need to build trust relationships, foster teamwork, and collaborate with and coach a variety of people. It stands to reason that self- and other-awareness, emotional self-management, and relationship skills are essential to success.

✓ In today's interconnected, complex and dynamic workplaces, managing relationships is perhaps more important, and more challenging than ever before.

✓ People with social intelligence tend to be approachable and outgoing. They promote cooperation and harmonious interactions with others. They build and value trust relationships that are mutually satisfying.

Enhance Your Learning

Watch this 2-minute video to help you better understand the relationship between emotional intelligence and social intelligence EQ and SQ:

Zito, W. (2012). *Emotional Intelligence Vs. Social Intelligence*.		Available at: https://www.youtube.com/watch?v=nZ3FAW103KU

Reinforce Your Learning

A. **Managing Relationships**. Imagine this scenario: You and a co-worker have been assigned to write a report for a client. Your co-worker, a member of your immediate work group, said that he had done something similar before and volunteered to draft the report. He assured you that he understood the specifications (report length, format, content and deadline). When you read the completed report, you find that it has serious issues that indicate your co-worker did not understand the specifications. The report is so bad that it needs to be totally redone and the client has been calling asking for it. You are very disappointed and frustrated.

Write out at least 5 steps that you could take to handle this situation without damaging the relationship with your co-worker.

B. **EI Applications for Managers**: Some of the key areas where emotional intelligence—from self-awareness through relationship management—plays a key role in managerial success are listed below. Take a few minutes and reflect on your own situation. In which of these areas would you like to express (or develop) greater emotional intelligence?

❑ Communicating a positive vision that inspires employees

❑ Securing support (inter-organizational or external/funder/regulator) through positive influence

❑ Creating a climate with a strong sense of team, shared responsibility, collaboration

❑ Providing feedback, coaching and positive discipline to help employees meet performance and behavioral expectations

❑ Leading in ways that support high levels of employee loyalty and engagement

❑ Supporting individual development through growth-oriented coaching, mentoring, recognition of the individual's needs for development

❑ Others:

EI Applications for Individual Contributors: In which of these areas do you want to express (or develop) greater emotional intelligence?

❑ Expressing your views and preferences in positive, inspiring ways

❑ Listening to others with understanding

❑ Influencing others to adopt an idea (or plan) that is very important to you

❑ Responding to interpersonal conflict in positive ways

❑ "Reading" the mood of the group

❑ Building agreement or consensus

❑ Others:

C. **Goleman's competency model** includes the following as part of relationship management. Take a minute or two and review the list and identify any of the competencies you would like to develop.

Relationship Management

Influence: Wielding effective tactics for persuasion. People with this competence:

- ❑ Are skilled at persuasion
- ❑ Fine-tune presentations to appeal to the listener
- ❑ Use complex strategies like indirect influence to build consensus and support
- ❑ Orchestrate dramatic events to effectively make a point

Leadership: Inspiring and guiding individuals and groups. People with this competence:

- ❑ Articulate and arouse enthusiasm for a shared vision and mission
- ❑ Step forward to lead as needed, regardless of position
- ❑ Guide the performance of others while holding them accountable
- ❑ Lead by example

Change Catalyst: Initiating or managing change. People with this competence:

- ❑ Recognize the need for change and remove barriers
- ❑ Challenge the status quo to acknowledge the need for change
- ❑ Champion the change and enlist others in its pursuit
- ❑ Model the change expected of others

Developing Others: Sensing what others need in order to develop and bolstering their abilities. People with this competence:

- ❑ Acknowledge and reward people's strengths, accomplishments and development
- ❑ Offer useful feedback and identify people's needs for development
- ❑ Mentor, give timely coaching, and offer challenging assignments

Conflict Management: Negotiating and resolving disagreements. People with this competence:

- ❑ Handle difficult people and tense situations with diplomacy and tact
- ❑ Spot potential conflict, bring disagreements into the open, and help deescalate tensions
- ❑ Encourage debate and open discussion to orchestrate win-win solutions

Teamwork and Collaboration: Working with others toward shared goals and creating group synergy in pursuing collective goals. People with this competence:

❑ Balance a focus on task with attention to relationships

❑ Collaborate, sharing plans, information and resources

❑ Spot and nurture opportunities for collaboration

❑ Model team qualities (respect, helpfulness, cooperation)

❑ Build team identity, team spirit and commitment

❑ Protect the group and its reputation; share credit

Note your reaction to the following statement: *An individual who has effective social intelligence skills can connect with associates, generate their trust and dedication, encourage them towards innovation and hard work, motivate them to success and development in their own career, and in short create happier, more effective associates.*

"Until you make the unconscious conscious, it will direct your life
and you will call it fate."

- C.G Jung

Promote an Emotionally Positive Work Climate

We have reviewed the value of emotional intelligence to your health, success and well-being in life, and how it helps you to work more productively with others: your co-workers, managers, customers and other associates. We examined the impact of negative emotions on behavior, and reviewed suggestions for increasing mindfulness to help you control impulsive behavior. We discussed the importance of developing your ability to treat situations and interactions in ways that promote more positive emotions and how these emotions contribute to personal growth and openness to new ideas. We have examined the importance of empathy, the key social competency, and explored some of the other social competencies that contribute to successful performance and peace of mind. We now want to look at what you can do to support a work climate that is emotionally positive for more people, more of the time.

Some work conditions –work overload, inadequate control or autonomy, rewards that are perceived to be inadequate, seemingly unrelenting change—increase the likelihood that employees will experience more negative than positive emotions. There is no doubt that these conditions often result from external or marketplace forces beyond the control of the supervisor or higher-level managers. There is also no doubt that emotionally intelligent leaders can help employees maintain high levels of performance and positive expectations even in the presence of less-than-ideal conditions. This efficacy seems rooted in how the leaders manage their interactions with direct reports, how they communicate vision and expectations, recognize performance, stimulate growth, build teams, and show empathy and respect even in challenging situations.

Following are some important things to keep in mind about supporting an emotionally positive work climate:

Positive interactions benefit relationships, performance and engagement and help reduce work-related stress.   When you express appreciation for a co-worker's helpful behavior or acknowledge someone's hard work in achieving a goal or meeting a deadline, or thank someone for their encouraging words, you are exemplifying what is meant by **positive interactions**. In theory, more positive than negative interactions contribute to a more positive work climate, which should boost employee engagement and retention. How much, and what ratio of positive to negative is most effective is up for question.

People differ from each other in many ways, including their need for positive affirmation and tolerance for challenging or negative feedback. While it seems reasonable that experiencing more positive than negative interactions would impact the work climate and people's emotions and performance positively, the reality is that "how much is needed" is not the same for everyone. The key is knowing your co-workers well enough that you can understand the balance that is important to motivating and engaging each of them. This understanding is especially important if you are in a position of leadership.

Think about your work climate and what you, personally, do to keep interactions positive. Consider:

- What do you do that compliments others –your peers and team members, your boss and others in management?

- Who has done something very helpful to you that you have not acknowledged or thanked? What do you want to do to express appreciation?

- Why might you sometimes not acknowledge what other people have done to help you achieve your results?

- Do you let your co-workers, and your immediate supervisor, know that you value your work relationship? That you count on their knowledge and support?

- Do you receive frequent compliments, statements of appreciation and offers of support from others? If not, why do you think this is the case?

Emotions are contagious. Remember mirror neurons. Both positive and negative emotions can affect us below our full conscious awareness. Be a carrier of positive, not negative emotions. Know when it is best for you to minimize interactions with others. It's perfectly okay to tell a co-worker that you need a bit more time, or more composure, before tackling a "thorny" issue. Just be sure you don't put it off hoping it will go away.

Emotions at Work. Think a bit about the emotions you experience in completing your work and do a quick assessment.

Directions: Using a scale of **1 (low)** to **9 (high)**, rate the degree to which you experience the following emotions during a workday. For example, a rating of **"1" for** *Fear* **would mean that you experience no or very little fear** during the course of a typical workday. **A rating of "9" for** *Happiness* **would mean that you experience happiness throughout the day.** Use the blanks at the end to add other emotions that you experience at work.

EMOTION	Rating								
Enthusiasm	1	2	3	4	5	6	7	8	9
Anger	1	2	3	4	5	6	7	8	9
Disappointment	1	2	3	4	5	6	7	8	9
Joy	1	2	3	4	5	6	7	8	9
Anxiety	1	2	3	4	5	6	7	8	9
Fear	1	2	3	4	5	6	7	8	9
Depression	1	2	3	4	5	6	7	8	9
Apathy	1	2	3	4	5	6	7	8	9
Happiness	1	2	3	4	5	6	7	8	9
Sadness	1	2	3	4	5	6	7	8	9
Surprise	1	2	3	4	5	6	7	8	9
Gratification	1	2	3	4	5	6	7	8	9
	1	2	3	4	5	6	7	8	9
	1	2	3	4	5	6	7	8	9

<u>Now respond to this question</u>:   What emotions do you think best characterize your current work environment? Consider, first, your personal emotions. Then consider how the emotional experience may be different at different levels and for different groups.

Take responsibility for your emotions, thoughts and behaviors. Be self-aware. Know which emotions you are experiencing and what triggers them. Take the time to consider what contributed to your experience of a positive or negative emotion. Do not underestimate the value of experiencing more positive emotions, more of the time. Negative emotions, such as fear and anger are legitimate emotions, and they push you to act. If you are not in physical danger, however, the after-effects of the emotional arousal doesn't help. If you behave impulsively, you can damage your reputation, your relationships, and your self-esteem.

Practice empathy. Take the time to really listen to others and to understand what they are feeling and what triggered those feelings. Recognize that people have different perspectives and expectations, based on different life experiences. Your role, as an empathic person, is to *understand* this: *not to judge* it. Your best clues about the emotional states of other people come from their facial expressions, body language and tone of voice.

Constantly work to improve your understanding of your own emotions and the emotions of others. Work on your emotional intelligence every day and take note of how your new behaviors are making a difference in your work and work relationships.

Periodically **evaluate** the status of your various **work relationships**. Consider which relationships would benefit the most from your more careful **application of EI**. Consider the following:

- Learn to **read your boss's moods** and respond accordingly, anticipating his or her needs.

- Learn **to listen to your associates** and work to understand their needs and values.

- Practice **anticipating the needs** and emotions of your **clients** and **customers**.

Before giving feedback to another person or attempting to resolve a conflict, it is a good idea to check your emotional or mood state. Because our behaviors, including how we communicate, are affected by our emotional state, it just makes sense to do a quick check-up before speaking. If your mood is not conducive to responding in respectful, positive, open ways, wait until it is (that is, unless the situation is one where the risk of not speaking is greater than the risk of misspeaking).

Let's look at one simple example of how applying emotional intelligence can improve a climate.

- You are in the checkout line at the office supply store. As you wait for the people in front of you, you notice that no one is really talking. The cashier is silently ringing up everyone's items, taking their credit cards, bagging the items, then moving to the next person. You hear one customer's sarcastic grumble as she walks away, "Thank you and have a nice day." "Great," you think, "I'm already running behind and now I have to deal with this poor customer service." Then, you check yourself. You realize that you are letting your perception of the cashier's behavior affect your emotions and how you are thinking. You take a deep breath and change your response.

- Placing your items on the counter you look up at the cashier, and in a very friendly voice say, "Hello." She mumbles something incoherent, but you press on. "How are you today?" "I'm okay," she replies. "Well," you say, "I hope you are getting off work soon, because it's a beautiful day out there." "Actually," says the cashier, a little friendlier now, "I still have four hours left in my shift." "Well," you make direct eye contact, smile and reply, still upbeat, "That's not too terrible – still plenty of daylight to enjoy at that point." She bags your items; you pick them up and say "Have a great day! I hope your four hours go quickly." The cashier says, somewhat brightly, "Thanks," and then you hear her address the next customer, "Hello sir. How are you today?"

- You smile – had you replied to the cashier in kind, matching her attitude, you might have been drawn into her negativity and you certainly wouldn't have had a positive effect on the climate. Instead, you decided to be polite and positive and helped change her attitude. If you can do that with a cashier imagine how your behavior could affect the people in your workplace.

EI will be increasingly of value in workplaces. According to one survey of hiring managers, 71% value EI higher than IQ, 59% will not hire a high IQ candidate if he or she lacks high EI, and 75% are more likely to promote an employee with high EI over one with high IQ (*Profiles International,* 2013).

What to do:	Other actions:
☐ Identify what you can do to improve the level of positivity in any weak or troubled relationships.	☐ _____
	☐ _____
☐ Make it a daily practice to look for opportunities to express your appreciation for your co-workers, and your respect for their knowledge, skills, and ideas.	☐ _____
	☐ _____
	☐ _____
☐ Observe your work climate for instances of positive and negative interactions.	☐ _____
	☐ _____

Remember

✓ Never underestimate the value of EI! As one psychologist put it, "Emotion can override thoughts, transform relationships, and profoundly influence behavior. Emotional intelligence allows us to harness that power to understand ourselves, overcome challenges, and build strong relationships" (Segal, n.d., para. 3).

✓ Positive interactions benefit relationships, performance and engagement and help reduce work-related stress. If the ratio in your workplace is from 3 to 6 positives to each negative, performance will be enhanced, and it is easier for people to become engaged.

Enhance Your Learning

Watch the following 15-minutes Ted Talk video to learn more about the importance of emotional intelligence in the workplace:

TEDx. (2016). *How We've Been Misled by 'Emotional Intelligence'*.		Available at: https://www.youtube.com/watch?v=6l8yPt8S2gE

Reinforce Your Learning

A. **Top Ten Suggestions (Hein, 2007).** Check your interest in any of the following suggestions for increasing your emotional intelligence:

Improvement Suggestion	Example
1. Become emotionally literate. Label your feelings rather than labeling people or situations. Analyze your own feelings rather than the actions or motives of others.	"I feel impatient." vs. "This is ridiculous." "I feel hurt and bitter." vs. "You are an insensitive jerk." "I feel afraid." vs. "You are driving like a maniac."
2. Distinguish between thoughts and feelings.	**Thoughts**: I would like, I prefer, I want, I don't want, I conclude. **Feelings**: I feel angry, sad, fearful, happy, disgusted, embarrassed.
3. Take more responsibility for your feelings. This means you will also have to make time to reflect on your feelings.	Stop believing others cause your feelings. Don't credit them with making you angry or hold them responsible for making you happy. Think and say: "I feel jealous." Instead of "You are making me jealous."
4. Use your feelings to help make decisions.	Ask: "How will I feel if I do this?" "How will I feel if I don't?" Develop the courage to follow your own feelings.
5. Show respect for other people's feelings.	Ask: "How will you feel if I do this?" "How will you feel if I don't?"
6. Feel energized, not angry.	Use what others call anger to help feel energized to take productive action.
7. Validate other people's feelings.	Show empathy, understanding and acceptance of other people's feelings.
8. Practice getting a positive value from emotions.	Ask yourself, "How do I feel?" and "What would help me feel better?"
9. Don't advise, command, control, criticize, judge, or lecture to others.	Instead, try to just listen with empathy and non-judgment.
10. Avoid people who invalidate you.	While this is not always possible, at least try to spend less time with them, or develop ways to reduce their psychological power over you.

Which suggestions would you like to follow to a greater extent than you currently do? **Circle the numbers for no more than three** of these suggestions and refer back to this page as you do your development plan.

B. **Plan ways** that you can **use emotional intelligence** to develop yourself further and improve your effectiveness in the workplace:

- Analyze your relationships.
- Practice EI by watching people every day.
- Keep a journal of your emotional triggers.
- Take a workshop or read a book in EI; you can never learn too much.
- Stay abreast of current research in EI.
- Use your EI skills to improve the effectiveness of employee orientations and evaluations.
- Use EI to help your associates to be more effective and embrace change.
- Use your EI to notice small issues in the workplace or with your associates before they become large problems.

Brainstorm **more ways** that you can apply EI in your workplace.

Summary

Emotional Competence Is Essential for Success in Today's Work Environments

Emotional competence enhances our personal, relational and professional performance and, ultimately, helps us achieve success and contentment in our professional and personal lives.

According to Daniel Goleman and other theorists, emotional competencies are learned, and development can continue throughout our lives. In this course, we examined the competencies using a four-category model: self-awareness, self-management, social awareness, and relationship management.

How we deal with our own emotions has a direct effect on how well we meet our work responsibilities and communicate with others. Being able to read, understand, and properly react to the emotions of others enables us to build trust relationships, influence and inspire others, and collaborate to solve problems and resolve conflicts.

Consider **what actions you can take** to improve your emotional intelligence and continue to apply your skills in the workplace and in your personal life. Ask yourself:

- Do I understand what emotional intelligence is and why it is important?

- Do I see any gaps in my emotional intelligence?

- What can I do every day to improve my use of emotional intelligence to build relationships?

- What should I do if I have questions about how my behavior affects others?

- Am I prepared to handle difficult situations that may arise in my work?

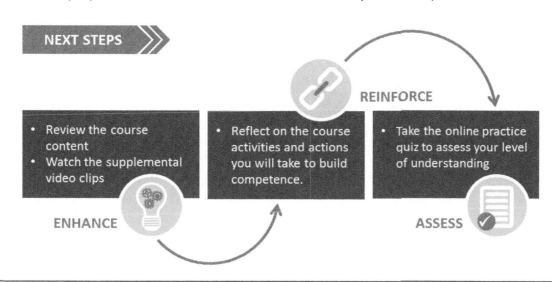

NEXT STEPS

REINFORCE

- Review the course content
- Watch the supplemental video clips

- Reflect on the course activities and actions you will take to build competence.

- Take the online practice quiz to assess your level of understanding

ENHANCE

ASSESS

Notes:

Enhancing Your Emotional Intelligence – Recap Checklist

Emotional intelligence has become a crucial component for building relationships in workplace environments. Reportedly, EI accounts for 58% of your success in life, professional and private; and only 36% of people are able to recognize their emotional state. Additionally, even if a person has a lower IQ than another person, they will outperform that smarter person seven out of ten times if the less intelligent person has a higher EI.

1. Define Emotional Intelligence and Understand its Benefits:
- ☐ Pay attention to how you respond to difficult or challenging interactions or work situations.
- ☐ Pay attention to how your co-workers respond when things are not going well.
- ☐ Consider how important emotional intelligence is in your workplace, and whether or not it is evident in workplace interactions.

2. Understand How the Brain Processes Emotions:
- ☐ Choose one emotion, such as anger or joy, and think about your behavior when feeling that emotion.
- ☐ Identify a situation in which you responded automatically and a situation in which you consciously chose your response. How were the results different?
- ☐ Identify one or mechanisms you use for calming down when emotions are getting out of control.

3. Describe How Positive and Negative Emotions Affect Behavior:
- ☐ Whenever you are in a non-physically threatening situation and sense a negative emotion, pull back and give yourself time to think of explanations that lead to more positive emotional responses.
- ☐ Work with another person to positively resolve a conflict, provide feedback, or solve a problem.
- ☐ Know whether you're in response to a challenge tends to be more optimistic or pessimistic.

4. Assess Your Emotional Intelligence Competencies:
- ☐ Review the list of EI competencies and give thought to how you might use them in your work.
- ☐ Assess your emotional intelligence using the competencies list or "six pillars" that were introduced.
- ☐ Based on the results from your EI assessment, identify competencies you will commit to developing.

5. Develop Emotional Self Awareness:
- ☐ Pay attention to the thoughts and physical conditions associated with your different feelings.
- ☐ After an emotionally arousing situation, think about what happened and record your responses.
- ☐ Ask someone you trust to give you feedback about how you respond in emotionally charged situations.

6. Develop Your Skills in Emotional Regulation:
- ☐ Recognize where you need to manage your impulsive behavior and decide how you will do so.
- ☐ Make a commitment to increase your self-management, in whatever area (i.e., body, thoughts, feelings, behavior) you consider most significant to your present situation.
- ☐ Work on replacing negative self-talk (and negative other-talk) with positive.

7. Read Other People's Emotions Effectively:
- ☐ Pay attention to how people are acting when they speak: voice, facial expression, body language.
- ☐ Get beyond your own emotions and tune in to what someone else is feeling.
- ☐ Observe people as they are talking together, looking for visible cues about their emotional states.

8. Support Others in Managing Their Emotions:
- ☐ Consider the effects of mirroring on the climate and use body language to signal positive emotions.
- ☐ Help others manage their emotions by acting to ensure that their core concerns are met reasonably.
- ☐ When you are trying to gain control of a situation, have ways to stay positive and keep your cool.

9. Identify Essential Social Intelligence Competencies:
- ☐ Recognize the importance of social intelligence, especially managing work relationships.
- ☐ Review the guidelines for managing work relationships and identify 1 or 2 that you will begin following.
- ☐ Choose one interaction where you will focus on being present throughout the interaction.

10. Promote an Emotionally Positive Work Climate:
- ☐ Identify what you can do to improve the level of positivity in any weak or troubled relationships.
- ☐ Make it a daily practice to look for opportunities to express your appreciation for your co-workers, and your respect for their knowledge, skills, and ideas.
- ☐ Observe your work climate for instances of positive and negative interactions.

Action Planning | **Competency #1** 〉〉

Self-Responsibility and Management
— *displays responsibility, self-confidence, emotional self-control, integrity, and honesty*

Briefly Describe how improvement in this competency will help you achieve important results or better meet your job responsibilities.

List courses, books, and independent study opportunities that could help you develop this competency.

Identify one or more people who could help you, either as a role model or source of information. Write any questions you want to ask each person

What specific steps will you take?	Start Date	Finished

Action Planning | **Competency #2** >> **Interpersonal Skills**
- appropriately Sociable; interacts Effectively with others

Briefly Describe how improvement in this competency will help you achieve important results or better meet your job responsibilities.

List courses, books, and independent study opportunities that could help you develop this competency.

Identify one or more people who could help you, either as a role model or source of information. Write any questions you want to ask each person

What specific steps will you take?	Start Date	Finished

Action Planning | **Competency #3** >>

Interpersonal Relationship Building
- considers and responds appropriately to needs, feelings, and capabilities of others; seeks feedback and accurately assesses impact on others; provides helpful feedback; builds trust with others

Briefly Describe how improvement in this competency will help you achieve important results or better meet your job responsibilities.

List courses, books, and independent study opportunities that could help you develop this competency.

Identify one or more people who could help you, either as a role model or source of information. Write any questions you want to ask each person

What specific steps will you take?	Start Date	Finished

"The greatest ability in business is to get along with others and influence their actions."

— John Hancock

Appendices

Appendix A: Knowledge Review Test

    Part 1: Knowledge Review Test – Answer Sheet

    Part 2: Knowledge Review Test - Questions

Appendix B: *Emotional Intelligence Self-Evaluation & Development Plan*

Appendix A: Part 1. Knowledge Review Test – Answer Sheet

Because It is not always convenient to take on-line courses, we now offer the option for you to earn Professional Development Units (PDHs) through a process like a correspondence course. You can study the content of this workbook at home or work, complete the following knowledge review test, and then fax, mail, or email the answer sheet along with the payment fee noted on our website. You can also copy and paste your answers below into our website Contact Form to submit them. We will then email your certificate of completion to you, or if you prefer, we can mail it.

Alternatively, you can register for courses at www.centrestar.com and work through the material online, take the test, and download your certificate.

Course: **Improving Your Emotional Intelligence** (CPE 2209)

Name:

Email:

Address:

I certify that I have completed this test myself. _____ Yes _____ No

Signature: _____ Date: _____

Circle or check the best answer to each question.

1.	___A	___B	___C	___D	___E
2.	___A	___B	___C	___D	___E
3.	___A	___B	___C	___D	___E
4.	___A	___B	___C	___D	___E
5.	___A	___B	___C	___D	___E
6.	___A	___B	___C	___D	___E
7.	___A	___B	___C	___D	___E
8.	___A	___B	___C	___D	___E
9.	___A	___B	___C	___D	___E
10.	___A	___B	___C	___D	___E
11.	___A	___B	___C	___D	___E
12.	___A	___B	___C	___D	___E
13.	___A	___B	___C	___D	___E
14.	___A	___B	___C	___D	___E
15.	___A	___B	___C	___D	___E
16.	___A	___B	___C	___D	___E
17.	___A	___B	___C	___D	___E
18.	___A	___B	___C	___D	___E
19.	___A	___B	___C	___D	___E
20.	___A	___B	___C	___D	___E

Appendix A: Part 2. Knowledge Review Test - Questions

CPE 2209 Improving Your Emotional Intelligence

1. Which of the following is true NOT true?
    A. EI is arguably more important than IQ.
    B. EI is short for emotional intelligence
    C. EI is short for social intelligence
    D. EQ = EI = emotional intelligence
    E. All of the above are true.

2. What part of the brain controls our emotions including the impulses towards fight, flight, or freeze?
    A. The gray matter
    B. The white matter
    C. The amygdala
    D. The cerebellum
    E. None of the above impact emotions.

3. Which of the following is NOT one of the four aspects of emotional intelligence?
    A. Self-management
    B. Self-awareness
    C. Self-regulation
    D. Self-motivation
    E. All of the above represent the four aspects

4. Emotional intelligence is important to being a good employee and family person, but it does not impact leadership skills.
    A. True
    B. False

5. Which of the following is the first step in demonstrating EI?
    A. Self-management
    B. Empathy
    C. Leadership
    D. Self-awareness
    E. None of the above are particularly important.

6. Management of your body, thoughts, feelings and behavior are part of what?
    A. Self-management
    B. Empathy
    C. Leadership
    D. Self-awareness
    E. None of the above

7. Being able to identify with and understand another person's feelings, that is being able to imagine yourself in their situation, is what?
>   A. Sympathy
>   B. EQ
>   C. Empathy
>   D. SQ
>   E. All of the above are true.

8. Pretending to show interest in a person is an effective way of demonstrating social intelligence.
>   A. True
>   B. False

9. What motivates a person?
>   A. Money
>   B. Emotions
>   C. Extrinsic factors
>   D. The amygdala
>   E. None of the above

10. What are the two basic types of motivation?
>   A. Emotional and logical
>   B. Intrinsic and extrinsic
>   C. Money and fear
>   D. Boss and spouse
>   E. None of the above

11. EI will be increasingly of value in workplaces.
>   A. True
>   B. False

12. Which of the following are basic emotions that have been found to be similarly expressed in different cultures.
>   A. Fear
>   B. Sadness
>   C. Anger
>   D. Surprise
>   E. All of the above

13. Giving in to another person by acknowledging that you were wrong, changing your opinion, or just letting the other person have their way, is a type of failure.

    A. True

    B. False

14. The term mindfulness means what?

    A. Using your brain more effectively

    B. Improving your EQ

    C. Being in the moment

    D. Improving your SQ

    E. All of the above are true

15. Which of the following is a great tool to get a person who totally disagrees with you seeing your way a bit using body language?

    A. Crossing your arms

    B. Mirroring

    C. Giving a tell

    D. All of the above

    E. None of the above

16. Which of the following is true about body language?

    A. How you say something, and your body language is as important as what you say.

    B. It is what you say that matters, not how you say it.

    C. Body language has not been sufficiently studied in people.

    D. All of the above are true.

    E. None of the above is true.

17. Which of the following is true?

    A. People with higher EI scores are better problem solvers.

    B. People with lower EI scores are better problem solvers.

    C. EI doesn't impact problem solving ability.

    D. Only IQ impacts problem solving ability.

18. Research findings indicate that emotional intelligence may account for your success in life, professional and private.

      A. True.

      B. False.

19. Which of the following are important in making a first impression?

      A. Dress appropriately and professionally.

      B. Be cheerful and friendly.

      C. Demonstrate genuine interest in the other person.

      D. Look into the person's eyes.

      E. All of the above are important.

20. Once you develop good emotional intelligence it is not something that you ever have to worry about again.

      A. True

      B. False

Emotional Intelligence
Self-Evaluation & Development Plan

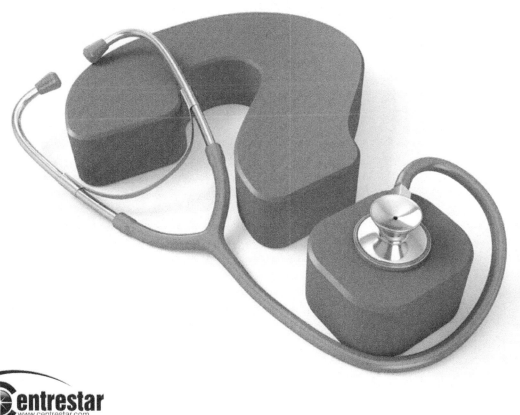

Centrestar
www.centrestar.com

Name: _____

Organization: _____

Date: _____

Introduction

Emotional intelligence involves the personal competencies of recognizing and managing our emotions, and the social competencies of recognizing others' emotions and managing our relationships. We all have some level of social intelligence, but the more you have the more effective you can be as an employee, a leader, a spouse, a parent and beyond.

The purpose of this self-evaluation and development plan is to measure your tendencies and abilities within various areas of emotional intelligence and then to plan your development activities for improving your competence, as necessary. The Emotional Intelligence Self-Evaluation measures five areas of emotional intelligence including:

1. Emotional Awareness

2. Managing Your Emotions

3. Self-Motivation

4. Empathy

5. Coaching Others' Emotions

In the pages below you will rate 30 statements based on your level of agreement. This is a survey of how well you know yourself, so feel free to answer quickly if the answer is obvious, or to take a moment to consider the answer if you are uncertain. But most importantly, be honest so that you can get accurate results that truly help you to improve yourself.

Once you score each statement you will be directed to add your scores and rank yourself in each of the five categories. Then you will have the opportunity to read about what your score in each section means. Finally, you will use this information, and a few open-ended questions, to create your own action plan to improve your emotional intelligence.

How much energy you put into the assessment and action plan will determine how well you improve your emotional intelligence to become a more effective leader.

Rating: In the space provided next to each of the following statements, please write in the number which best describes your agreement with the item, using the scale below.

1	2	3	4	5	6
Disagree Very Much	Disagree Moderately	Disagree Slightly	Agree Slightly	Agree Moderately	Agree Very Much

---

1 - Disagree very much	2	3	4	5	6 - Agree very much

1. _____ I use both negative and positive emotions as a source of wisdom about how to navigate my life.

2. _____ Negative feelings help me to address what I need to change in my life.

3. _____ I am calm under pressure.

4. _____ I have the ability to monitor my feelings from moment to moment.

5. _____ When challenged, I am good at getting calm and focused to flow with life's demands.

6. _____ When challenged, I am able to summon a wide range of positive emotions such as fun, joy, fighting spirit, and humor.

7. _____ I am in charge of how I feel.

8. _____ After something has upset me, I find it easy to regain my composure.

9. _____ I am effective at listening to other people's problems.

10. _____ I do not recycle and dwell on negative emotions.

11. _____ I am sensitive to the emotional needs of others.

12. _____ I have a calming influence on other people.

13. _____ I am able to motivate myself to try and try again in the face of setbacks.

14. _____ I try to be creative with life's challenges.

15. _____ I respond appropriately to other people's moods, motivations, and desires.

16. _____ I can easily enter into a "zone" state, or a state characterized by calmness, alertness, and focus.

17. _____ When the time is right, I face my negative feelings and work through what the issue is.

18. _____ I am capable of soothing myself after an upsetting event.

19. _____ Knowing my true feelings is crucial to my well-being.

20. _____ I am good at understanding the emotions of other people, even when the emotions are not directly expressed.

21. _____ I am adept at reading people's feelings by their facial expressions.

22. _____ I can easily set negative feelings aside when called upon to perform.

23. _____ I am aware of subtle social signals that indicate what others need.

24. _____ People view me as an effective coach for others' emotions.

25. _____ People who are aware of their true feelings are better pilots of their lives.

26. _____ I am often able to improve the moods of others.

27. _____ I am a good person to come to for advice about handling relationships.

28. _____ I am strongly attuned to others' feelings.

29. _____ I help others use their motivations to achieve their personal goals.

30. _____ I can easily shake off negative feelings.

Note: Self-evaluation statements were developed by Dr. Nicholas Hall; permission to reproduce given by Salum International Resources.

Scoring: Transfer your scores for each item as indicated; add to get your total for each area.

Emotional Awareness

1. _____ I use both negative and positive emotions as a source of wisdom about how to navigate my life.

2. _____ Negative feelings help me to address what I need to change in my life.

4. _____ I have the ability to monitor my feelings from moment to moment.

17. _____ When the time is right, I face my negative feelings and work through what the issue is.

19. _____ Knowing my true feelings is crucial to my well-being.

25. _____ People who are aware of their true feelings are better pilots of their lives.

_____ **Total Emotional Awareness**

Managing Your Emotions

3. _____ I am calm under pressure.

7. _____ I am in charge of how I feel.

8. _____ After something has upset me, I find it easy to regain my composure.

10. _____ I do not recycle and dwell on negative emotions.

18. _____ I am capable of soothing myself after an upsetting event.

30. _____ I can easily shake off negative feelings.

_____ **Total Managing Your Emotions**

Self-Motivation

5. _____ When challenged, I am good at getting calm and focused to flow with life's demands.

6. _____ When challenged, I am able to summon a wide range of positive emotions such as fun, joy, fighting spirit, and humor.

13. _____ I am able to motivate myself to try and try again in the face of setbacks.

14. _____ I try to be creative with life's challenges.

16. _____ I can easily enter into a "zone" state, or a state characterized by calmness, alertness, and focus.

22. _____ I can easily set negative feelings aside when called upon to perform.

_____ **Total Self-Motivation**

Empathy

9. _____ I am effective at listening to other people's problems.

11. _____ I am sensitive to the emotional needs of others.

20. _____ I am good at understanding the emotions of other people, even when the emotions are not directly expressed.

21. _____ I am adept at reading people's feelings by their facial expressions.

23. _____ I am aware of subtle social signals that indicate what others need.

28. _____ I am strongly attuned to others' feelings.

_____ **Total Empathy**

Coaching Others' Emotions

12. _____ I have a calming influence on other people.

15. _____ I respond appropriately to other people's moods, motivations, and desires.

24. _____ People view me as an effective coach for others' emotions.

26. _____ I am often able to improve the moods of others.

27. _____ I am a good person to come to for advice about handling relationships.

29. _____ I help others use their motivations to achieve their personal goals.

_____ **Total Coaching Others' Emotions**

Record your scores for each competency area here:

Emotional Awareness	Managing Your Emotions	Self-Motivation	Empathy	Coaching Others' Emotions

Interpret your Results: Comparing your scores with the chart below allows you to assess your current standing on the various emotional competencies relative to a cross-industry sampling of managers and other professionals.

Emotional Competency	Definite Strength	Need Some Development	Need Substantial Development
Emotional Awareness	31 or above	26 – 30	25 or below
Managing Your Emotions	32 or above	27 – 31	25 or below
Self-Motivation	31 or above	27 – 30	26 or below
Empathy	31 or above	26 – 30	25 or below
Coaching Others' Emotions	30 or above	25 – 29	24 or below

Interpreting Your Profile

You may be looking at your scores and wondering what you should do now. Perhaps your scores are lower than you expected – what might this mean? What if you scored really high – do you need to do anything?

Perhaps you scored really well in most of these areas, and only low in one or two. Or, maybe you are feeling that emotional intelligence is certainly not your strong suit because you scored extremely low in all five areas. Not to fear. No matter how many areas you identified as requiring growth, the good news is that these are all learnable behaviors. In fact, with some work, you can soon achieve higher emotional intelligence scores.

Let's look a bit at the meaning of your scores in each of the five areas and help you to better understand your score. Then we will move on to helping you create your specific development plan. As you read the descriptions below look at your score and keep in mind whether you scored low, average or high in each area and what that may mean.

Emotional Awareness.

Emotional Awareness considers how well you recognize and understand your own emotions and those of others around you. When we are aware of our own emotions, we can recognize what our emotions are without letting them control us. For example, when a worker does something wrong on the job that causes a problem, you should be able to identify your emotional reaction: disappointed, worried, sad, angry or some other emotion. Properly recognizing your emotions can help you to monitor and regulate your behavior to ensure the best possible outcome, or at least avoid creating new problems.

The same is true of recognizing emotions within others. If a customer begins yelling at you over a problem, take the time to consider what emotion is driving them. If you assume they are angry you may react back in an angry way, simply masking the real problem. If you take the time to listen and be emotionally aware you might realize that the customer is not just angry, they are actually scared, nervous, stressed, or some other emotion. Understanding that can help you to react better and more productively manage the situation.

Emotionally aware people reflect upon their own feelings and those of others, working to label and understand their emotions. People with high emotional awareness are able to identify their own emotions and use that knowledge to better understand the situation and manage their behaviors. These people monitor their emotions in different situations, evaluating how they feel from moment to moment. They learn to separate their emotions from the situation and view them through a more objective lens.

People with high emotional awareness also have the ability to (and take the time to) recognize the true emotions that are guiding the behaviors of others. They know that identifying emotional states is the first step towards understanding situations and making positive decisions or improving relationships.

People with low emotional awareness will not take the time or energy to evaluate their own emotions. They react without identifying their own motivations, and often make matters worse by overreacting or reading situations incorrectly. The inability of these people to be aware of their own emotions sends them spiraling down a path where they cannot manage their emotions, limiting their ability to effectively communicate with others and be productive.

If you scored low in emotional awareness do not be upset. You are not alone; many people have simply not taught themselves to analyze their own emotions. As the cliché goes, simply recognizing that you have a problem is the first step towards growth. When you get to the development plan below you will have an opportunity to list ways that you can help yourself to better connect with your own emotions and recognize the motivating emotions of others.

People with good emotional awareness:
- Recognize that understanding their emotions is an important part of their own well-being
- Identify both negative and positive emotions as sources of wisdom when navigating life
- Are able to monitor their own emotions from moment to moment
- Use negative feelings to spark change
- Better understand people around them

Managing Your Emotions.

If you scored low in emotional awareness then there is a good chance that you scored low in this section on Managing Your Emotions as well, because to truly manage your emotions you must first recognize them. Managing your emotions refers to how well you are able to not simply acknowledge your own emotions, but to control them.

When people manage their emotions, they are able to self-regulate and to impact their own behavior. For example, say that a client's computer system experienced an error that caused them to miss placing an order for supplies from your company that they desperately need. The client calls you and begins screaming at you about this problem, a problem that really isn't your fault. You are being screamed at, so you become angry.

Because you are emotionally aware, you realize that you are getting angry. But then, instead of giving in to your baser instinct and lashing out at the client, you manage your emotions. You take a deep breath, reign in your temper, and listen to the customer then calmly begin working on a solution. You don't let your anger control you and ruin this interaction. As a side note, your ability to be aware of emotions also helps you realize that this client is frustrated, and possibly scared, and that has nothing to do with what you have or have not done.

People with the ability to manage their emotions know how to recognize the emotion they are feeling, decide how valid or valuable it is, and then change their behavior accordingly. That is not to say that they stop the emotion – we can rarely accomplish this. Rather, the person is able to control the emotion in a way that doesn't let it negatively impact their behavior.

People who struggle to manage their emotions tend to get into a lot of conflict. These are often people who overreact, lash out in anger, say hurtful things, or later regret their actions or words. In our personal lives, the inability to manage emotions can lead to conflict, difficulty with interpersonal relationships, divorce, parenting struggles and so forth. In the workplace, it can lead to losing the respect of clients, peers and leaders, and a variety of other failures, even loss of one's job.

Fortunately, managing one's emotions is a learned behavior. Once one masters the concept of identifying their emotions, a person can easily move on to managing their emotions, learning to take the time to make careful, calculated decisions about their behavior.

People who manage their emotions:

- Can stay calm under pressure
- Can regain their composure when bad things happen
- Do not dwell on negative emotions
- Make better decisions based on facts rather than emotions

Self-Motivation.

Self-Motivation refers to the ability to not just recognize and then control your emotions, but to engage your emotions in a way that lets you get things done. A person with a high level of self-motivation is often more accomplished, and even happier. These people are self-directed, proactive, and productive.

People with high self-motivation tend to be more accomplished and less stressed. They see themselves in control of their own accomplishments and success. They know that how they behave makes a difference in their relationships, that it gets them results. Self-motivated people are often confident, respected leaders.

People who lack self-motivation tend to look to blame others when things go wrong. These people are not always respected, are rarely considered dependable authorities in their area, and may struggle to climb the corporate ladder or simply to accomplish their own personal and professional goals.

Some people seem to be born with a high level of self-motivation. These people are go-getters from day one, wanting to be independent and proactive. However, not all self-motivated people are born that way. Is it a skill that can be developed over time. If you scored low on self-motivation you will have an opportunity to list actionable ways of working on this skill in your development plan.

People who are self-motivated:

- Approach life's challenges creatively
- Can remain calm and positive in the face of challenges
- Can motivate themselves to try again after setbacks
- Can better focus and get things done

Empathy.

Empathy allows you to not only recognize the emotions of others, but to put yourself in their proverbial shoes and understand how they feel. Sympathy means acknowledge that someone has an emotion and feeling bad for them, but empathy implies truly understanding their emotion, creating within yourself some sense of how they must feel, and then demonstrating that understanding in a way that improves your communication and relationships.

People with high levels of empathy are able to connect with people on a deep level that forges relationships. They know how to treat people in a way that creates instant rapport, but also creates feelings of confidence and respect. As a leader, having empathy can help you to better understand your employees and your clients, creating more successful and beneficial relationships.

People who lack or fail to display empathy can struggle in creating relationships. Leaders who lack empathy find it difficult to get people to follow them. An example of a leader who lacked empathy was the fictional Dicken's character Ebenezer Scrooge. His lack of empathy may have helped him become wealthy, but it led to a very unsatisfying life for him and his underlings.

If you scored low on empathy do not worry. This doesn't make you a Scrooge. However, you will want to work on developing your empathy so that you can be a more effective leader, role model, employee, spouse and parent. Having good empathy skills will improve all areas of your life and is an important part of managing yourself and coaching other's emotions. People with good empathy:

- Are effective listeners
- Effectively read facial expressions and body language
- Understand the emotional needs of others

Coaching Other's Emotions.

Now we come to the final section of the assessment – Coaching Other's Emotions. When it comes to Coaching Other's Emotions, we do not mean that you behave as a psychologist and help people to understand their own emotions. Rather, this is about role modeling emotional control and helping to create an emotionally healthy environment around you.

Imagine that you woke up this morning in a great mood. Your coffee tasted extra good. The sun was shining. You simply felt great. You went to work, happy as you could be. Then, as you walked in the door, your boss barked out some grouchy orders, and you could see that everyone in the office looked stress and unhappy. Consider how quickly your happy mood might deflate under these conditions.

Consider this: Would you have accomplished more that day if you had arrived to work and remained in your happy mood? Or would you accomplish more in your unhappy, stressed state? The former, right? Certainly, most people get more done when they are cheerful and feeling good.

Now, imagine it in reverse. Imagine that you woke up with a pain in your neck. Then, you spilled your coffee and had a disagreement with your spouse. You arrive to work in a foul mood. But then your boss walks up and claps you on the back, wishing you a cheerful good morning and praising you for something you had done the day before. How do you feel now? How might your productivity be impacted?

People with a high ability to coach other's emotions are able to give a gift to other people in the form of better emotions. These people help others feel cheerful when they appear to be down. They can help install confidence in those who lack it. They can give hope to those who are wavering. This is not to say they can fix everything but helping others to modify their emotions in a more positive way can have a huge impact on an organization.

This ability to use social awareness and self-awareness to create better interactions with others and even to impact the emotional state of others is perhaps the rarest skill of the five we have discussed here. But it is not any more difficult. As with all of these skills it simply requires being aware of your own emotions and those of others, practicing empathy, controlling your emotions, being self-motivated, and then working to model and coach these skills in others.

People who can coach the emotions of others:

- Respond appropriately to the emotions, moods and needs of others
- Have a calming influence on other people
- Are viewed positively by others
- Are seen as people to go to for advice
- Help others to achieve their goals

Moving Forward

Now that you better understand your own score within these five emotional intelligence areas, it is time to create your own development plan. Each one of these areas are places where you can improve, no matter your score..

The following section will help you to clearly identify these areas and brainstorm some specific ways that you can improve. As you create your action plan feel free to spend a few minutes online researching suggestions for exercises that you can perform to improve in your problem areas. You may also wish to keep a journal as you move forward with your development plan, logging each day what you did to improve in a certain area and what improvements you are seeing.

Plan for Development

Part A: Your emotional intelligence strengths

1. In what competency area did you score highest?

2. Review your responses to the items related to that competency and indicate the specific skills or behaviors that represent your strengths. You may list the item numbers or abbreviated statements.

   a.

   b.

   c.

3. Briefly describe how you see these strengths benefiting you in your performance and work relationships?

4. How might you expand your use of these skills and behaviors?

Part B: Your emotional development needs

1. Decide which competency area you want to focus on first. Review your responses to the items related to that competency and select no more than 3 specific skills or behaviors you want to strengthen.

   Competency Area:

   Skills/Behaviors to Strengthen (item number or abbreviated statement):

   a.

   b.

   c.

2. How do you think development in these skills/behaviors will enhance your overall performance, job satisfaction or work relationships?

3. Note any initial ideas you have about what you might do to develop these skills/behaviors.

4. Who can you ask to give you feedback and reinforcement as you work to develop your skills?

Give yourself ample time to develop in the initial competency area, then select another area to concentrate on. You may want to do another self-assessment, or simply revisit the results from this assessment. Based on what you know now, which competency area will you most likely want to develop next?

Action Planning | I plan to: >>

Action Planning I plan to:

Sources/Citations

About Human Emotions, 2016 List of Human Emotions. Retrieved from: http://www.listofhumanemotions.com/

Akers, M. & Porter, G. (2016). *What is emotional intelligence?* Retrieved from: http://psychcentral.com/lib/what-is-emotional-intelligence-eq/

Bradberry, T. (2014). *Emotional intelligence – EQ.* Forbes. Retrieved from: http://www.forbes.com/sites/travisbradberry/2014/01/09/emotional-intelligence/#3beebe1a3ecb

Cherniss, G. (1999). *The business case for emotional intelligence.* Retrieved from: http://www.eiconsortium.org/research/business_case_for_ei.htm

Cherniss, G. (2000). *Emotional intelligence: What it is and why it matters.* Presentation at the Society for Industrial and Organizational Psychology annual meeting, New Orleans, LA, April 15, 2000. Retrieved from: http://www.eiconsortium.org/research/what_is_emotional_intelligence.htm

Cherniss, C., Goleman, D., & Emmerling, R. (1998*). A technical report issued by CREIO*, Retrieved from: http://www.eiconsortium.org/pdf/technical_report.pdf, pp. 5–6.

CREIO Newsletters. The Consortium for Research on Emotional Intelligence in Organizations (CREIO) regularly posts research studies and other information about emotional intelligence at http://www.eiconsortium.org.

Crompton, M. (2010). *Increase your emotional intelligence through self-management.* Retrieved from: http://www.peoriamagazines.com/ibi/2010/jun/increase-your-emotional-intelligence-through-self-management

Emmerling, R. J. & Goleman, D. (October 2003). *Emotional intelligence: Issues and common misunderstandings*, The Consortium for Research on Emotional Intelligence in Organizations. Retrieved from: http://www.eiconsortium.org.

Fisher, R & Shapiro, D. (2005). *Beyond reason: Using emotions as you negotiate.* NY: Viking, Penguin Group.

Fralich, T. (2005). *Through the path of mindfulness,* workshop conducted for PESI Health Care, Workshop manual, p 28, permission to use given by the author.

Fredrickson, B. (2000). *Cultivating positive emotions to optimize health and well-being, Prevention and treatment*, 3. Retrieved from: http://www.unc.edu//peplab/publciations/cultivating.pdf

Fredrickson, B. (2013). *Positive emotions broaden and build*, in Devine, P. & Plant, A. (ed) *Advances in Experimental Social Psychology, Volume 47.* San Diego, CA: Elsevier Science, 3-54.

Griffith, J. (2021). *Emotional Intelligence 2.0.* Independently published.

Goleman, D. (1995). *Emotional Intelligence.* New York: Bantam Books.

Goleman, D. (2019). Emotional Intelligence: For a Better Life, success at work, and happier relationships. Independently published.

Hay Group. (n.d.). *Emotional and social competency inventory (ESCI).* Available from:, http://www.haygroup.com/leadershipandtalentondemand/ourproducts/item_details.aspx?itemid=58&type=1

Hein, S.(2007) *Developing Emotional Intelligence: Top Ten Suggestions.* Available from: http://eqi.org/summary.htm, posted May 14, 2007.

Jennings, K. (n.d.). *6 ways to raise your emotional intelligence (EQ).* Retrieved from: http://www.lifehack.org/articles/communication/ways-raise-your-emotional-intelligence.html

Lyubomirsky, S., Sheldon, K.M., & Schkade, D. (2005). *Pursuing happiness: The architecture of sustainable change. Review of General Psychology*, 9, 111-131.

Malone, P. (2021). *Emotional Intelligence in Talent Development.* Association for Talent Development.

Ouspensky, P. D. (1954). *The psychology of man's possible evolution.* New York: Alfred A. Knopf

Peterson, C., Seligman, M.E.P. & Vaillant, GE. (1988) *Pessimistic explanatory style is a risk factor for physical illness: A thirty-five-year longitudinal study. J Pers Soc Psych*, 55, pp 23 – 27.

Peterson, C. & Vaidya, R.S. (2001). *Explanatory style, expectations and depressive symptoms. Pers Individ Dif.* 31, p 159-162

Profiles International Webinar, Feb. 2013

Psychology Today. (n.d.). *Emotional intelligence test.* Available from: http://psychologytoday.tests.psychtests.com/take_test.php?idRegTest=3203

Segal, J. (n.d.). *EQ: Emotional intelligence toolkit.* Retrieved from: http://www.helpguide.org/emotional-intelligence-toolkit/

Sheldon, O. J., Cunning, D., & Ames, D. R. (2014). *Emotionally unskilled, unaware, and uninterested in learning more: Reactions to feedback about deficits in emotional intelligence. Journal of Applied Psychology, 99* (1), 125–137.

Spradling, G. (n.d.) *The Four types of self-management skills we all really need.* Retrieved from, http://www.drgeorgiana.com/need-higher-self-management-skills/

Stein, s.J. Papadogiannis, P., Yip, J.A. & Sitarenios, G (2009). *Emotional intelligence of leaders: A profile of top executives. Leadership and Organization Development Journal*, 30 (1), 87-101.

Van Camp, E. (2015). *10 Emotional Intelligence facts that will blow you away!* LinkedIn. Retrieved from: https://www.linkedin.com/pulse/10-astonishing-ei-facts-eric-van-camp

Walton, D. (2012). *Emotional intelligence: A practical guide.* NY: MJF Books. (p 3 in concept 1)

All graphics purchased from Depositphotos.com (https://depositphotos.com/license.html).

Index

[Created with **TExtract** /
    www.TExtract.com]

About the Authors

Wesley E. Donahue, Ph.D.

As an engineer, manager, business owner, and now an educator, I have traveled to over 24 countries and 49 states, helping other people succeed. But like you, at each step of the way I had to learn, and I had to put that learning into action. This workbook speaks from the voice of experience.

As for my background, I earned a B.S. in Engineering from Penn State University, an M.B.A. from Clarion University, a Ph.D. in Workforce Education from Penn State, and am a professor at Penn State. In this capacity, I am engaged in top-ranked graduate research and programing in learning and performance, lead a successful online graduate program in organization development and change, and teach education and engineering courses. I am also President of Centrestar, Inc., a firm that produces and delivers competency-based courses for professionals.

Before that, I was Director of Penn State Management Development Programs and Services. We provided education and training services to business and industry clients around the world. Prior to that, I had years of experience as a project manager, manager, and business owner. I was Regional Sales Vice President for Mark-Kay Plastics in Kansas City, Missouri; co-founder and Executive Vice President of Leffer Systems of New Jersey, a manufacturing company; and International Manager of Technology for Brockway, Inc., a Fortune 200 company. I also co-owned and operated a retail business for over ten years.

I am a registered professional engineer; professional land surveyor; six-sigma black belt; certified project management professional; co-author of *Creating In-house Sales Training and Development Programs;* and author of:
- *Building Leadership Competence: A Competency-Based Approach to Building Leadership Ability,*
- *Unlocking Lean Six Sigma: A Competency-Based Approach to Applying Continuous Process Improvement Principles and Best Practice,*
- *Professional Ethics: A Competency-Based Approach to Understanding and Appling Professional Ethics.*
- *Fostering Diversity, Equity, and inclusion in the Workplace: A Competency-Based Approach to Building a Cohesive and Profitable Organization*

Katheryn K. Woodley, Ph.D.

I first became interested in human behavior, multiple intelligences and learning theory as an undergraduate psychology major. I intended to go into Clinical Psychology, but soon discovered that my temperament was better suited to working with people who were, from a diagnostic perspective, considered normal. And, because Akron University had just started a graduate program in Industrial Psychology, that seemed a natural fit for me. As part of my internship, I assisted my adviser in his work evaluating corporate human resource systems and practices, and assessing the intellectual, psychological and personality characteristics of candidates for leadership positions. This experience reinforced my interest in working to create more healthful workplaces: designing systems that support the mental, emotional and physical health of employees and ensuring that people in leadership positions are "fit to lead."

Katheryn K. Woodley, Ph.D. *(continued)*

A couple of career turns allowed me to build proficiency in instructional design and adult learning and gave me experience in supervising others. I made another career shift when I started, on a part-time basis, designing and conducting workshops for women in management. This ultimately led me to full time employment with Penn State's Management Development faculty. Along the way, I completed my PhD in Industrial-Organizational Psychology and obtained a PA Psychologist license.

During my over 30 years' experience at Penn State, I maintained a large external client base and provided internal support to the unit as point person for program design and development. I was involved in developing, or leading project teams to develop, training programs, workshops and other interventions covering virtually all management, interpersonal and personal mastery topics. Many programs were designed for multiple groups and levels, in order to facilitate organization-wide change. Many, including those dealing with emotional intelligence, focused on building positive work relationships and high-engagement work climates.

Employment Brief

- Westinghouse Learning Corporation: Supervisor, Project Plan Performance Standards
- The American College: Director of Instructional Design & Development
- The Pennsylvania State University: Member. Management Development faculty
- Woodley Associates: Leadership Development Consultant

Education and Professional Licenses & Certifications

- BA, Psychology, University of Akron
- MA, Industrial Psychology, University of Akron
- PhD, Industrial-Organizational Psychology, Union Graduate School
- PA Licensed Psychologist (1977-2017)
- MBTI® Qualified Practitioner
- Clark Wilson Task Cycle® Surveys
- Checkpoint 360® (Profiles International)
- Emotional Competence Inventory® (Hay Group)
- Qualified to administer Class B and C Psychological tests

We would enjoy hearing from you and learning how this workbook has helped you achieve your goals. Please contact us at wdonahue@centrestar.com